"Throughout this book, Rachel explores finding freedom in every aspect of her life. Rachel shares intimate parts of her story that God redeemed and restored. Rachel breaks down the root of destructive cycles and redirects to the Word of God as she recognizes that God is the only true key to find freedom. Not only is her story powerful, but the practical principles in this book can help others find that same freedom!!"

-Nancy Alcorn, Founder & President of Mercy Multiplied

"*Finding Freedom* by Rachel will captivate you from the moment you start reading. Her personal testimony of Jesus delivering her from addiction and a destructive lifestyle is a powerful story of restoration and redemption. If you are caught up in an addiction or you love someone who is, this book will both encourage and inspire you to believe that with God nothing is impossible! I highly recommend this book! I know it will bless you as much as it blessed me! Rachel is a living testimony of God's love and grace and that He is faithful to His promises!"

-Connie Witter, Because of Jesus Ministries

"Any person who has struggled with a drug addiction personally or within their family needs to read this book. Rachel not only shares her personal story of being delivered from drug addiction, but gives a lot of insight about the hurts, insecurities and other difficulties addicts often struggle with.

D1405823

The book is full of boundaries and practical steps that can help addicts and their families learn that there are ways to stop the destruction and hurt caused by addiction. Powerful and relevant!"

-Susie Barnes, President and Executive Director Glory House Tulsa, a Restoration Program for women

"*Finding Freedom* is a heart-wrenching, uplifting story of how God redeems the brokenhearted. Rachel's story of abuse—mental, physical, and emotional—does not usually come with a happy ending. Everything she tried fell apart in her hands. But God... woven throughout each chapter of hurt and loss is the scarlet thread of God's loving pursuit of this amazing young woman. Rachel shares her struggles in a real, but gentle way, neither shying away from the truth, nor glorifying the past. She offers hope even in the dark times and provides prayer and resources for those who are struggling too. Best of all, Rachel's life today is a testimony of complete restoration. I have seen the blessing and faithfulness of God in her life as she "walks the walk" in strength, grace, and integrity today."

-Lisa Taylor, Coordinator for Christian Caregiving and Counseling, Oral Roberts University

"Wow! This was a candid, powerful, practical, and genuine showcase of vulnerability and authenticity! *Finding Freedom* is a beacon of hope to the lives of women who find themselves stuck in the painful cycles of addiction, codependency, dysfunctional and abusive relationships, anxiety, self-injury, and depression. Rachel provides an approach to recovery from a lifestyle of addiction that uncompromisingly embraces both faith-based and mental health counseling interventions for healing. In her story, I find so many of the interventions I work on with my community mental health clients who suffer from domestic violence, substance abuse, and other addictions. Practicing vulnerability, creating structure, noticing red flags, saying no and setting healthy boundaries, recognizing triggers of persons, places, or things, creating accountability, identifying and changing negative beliefs are a few that anyone in recovery will recognize she practiced well. I would recommend this book to any of my clients who have been in and out of treatments and are searching for a way to integrate their rehab program with their faith and scripture-based truths. So many of our mental health programs do not or cannot include faith-based interventions; Rachel's book will help my faith-filled clients to dig deeper and lean stronger on this missing piece and inspire them as they uncover God's promise for their path to freedom from addiction and despair."

-Yasmine Alvarado, M.A., LMFT-C

"Rachel gives a glimpse into a life many won't understand. For those who have lived or are living the nightmares she relives in this book, there is hope. She points the way beautifully to the healer and proves with her life now that you can not only survive but thrive. I am someone who experienced childhood abuse and believe this book will be an excellent tool for anyone trying to find their way to healing."

-Mary Painter, Oklahoma Department of Corrections Volunteer Chaplain, Dr. Eddie Warrior Corrections Center

"Ever since meeting Rachel as a student at Victory College, I knew God had a profound call on her life. Her desire to love God & love people are evidence that God can rewrite anyone's story. Her journey to freedom is truly a trophy of God's grace. As I read through these pages I continued to think about John 8:32, "And you will know the truth, and the truth will set you free."

This book is filled with truth and refreshing transparency that will provide the keys to finding freedom that so many of us need and desire. Her story will inspire you to walk closer to Jesus, while giving practical application to find freedom from bitterness, addiction, confusion, and pain.

I was once someone lost and broken in similar ways to Rachel. I was without vision, without hope, and without joy, but then, Jesus. Get ready because *Finding Freedom* is about to give you the tools to find the life you were born to live."

-Pastor Mark Kresge, Executive Director, Victory College
Tulsa, OK

"I had no idea the young lady who sat down for the first time in my classroom at Victory Bible College a few years ago carried with her so much healed pain and hopeful passion. Since that first class, I've not only been Rachel's professor, I've had the privilege of seeing her in the professional world and serving with her on a mission trip to Ecuador.

Knowing what I know now, I can tell you that every word in this book is written from the heart of a woman of God who wants nothing more than to see God do for you what He did for her…and so much more! Rachel's story is raw and real and powerful. All of us struggle with something, and all of us need to know that there is hope. I am confident that this story, this message of hope, will not only bless you but every life that has the opportunity to read these pages. But don't just read this book. Stop along the way and read the Scriptures, pray the prayers, and make the decisions. In doing so, you will not only be blessed by Rachel's story, you will create your own through which God can continue His work of Amazing Grace."

-Nathan Faught, Professor at Victory Bible College, Vice President of Development at Success Vision, Tulsa, OK

"Rachel's story is a transformational map for anyone going through a difficult season. Her story will inspire you to believe that God is always chasing you even when you're running away from Him. As you read this book, I believe the stories found therein will cause hope to rise and fear to leave. What God did for Rachel, He will do for you! Be inspired. Let faith arise. And sit in awe of what Jesus is able to do."

-Joshua Wagner, Wagner Ministries International

Finding Freedom

A DRUG ADDICT'S STORY FROM DEATH TO LIFE

RACHEL DICK

Finding Freedom
Copyright © 2020 by Rachel Dick
All rights reserved.

No part of this publication may be reproduced, stored in
a retrieval system or transmitted in any way or by any
means, electronic, mechanical, photocopy, recording or
otherwise without the prior written permission of the au-
thor except as provided by USA copyright law.

Unless otherwise indicated, all Scripture quotations are
taken from the Holy Bible, New Living Translation, copyright © 1996, 2004, 2015 by Tyndale House Foundation.
Used by permission of Tyndale House Publishers, Inc.,
Carol Stream, Illinois 60188. All rights reserved.

Details in some anecdotes and stories have been changed
to protect the identities of the persons involved.

Cover design & Layout design by Kaycee Tattershall
Editing by Bethany Duarte

Published in the United States of America
ISBN: 978-0-578-70165-3

*To my family that relentlessly pursued
my freedom and never gave up on me*

Table of Contents

Introduction

As I laid in bed one night, desperate, lonely, and depressed, I started to cry. I cried so hard I could barely catch my breath.

My boyfriend and I had just finished a week bender, and all the drugs and money were gone. Mentally, I was in a really dark place, the darkest place I had been in a while. My thoughts were consumed with hopelessness and helplessness. I truly believed that I was going to be depressed for the rest of my life. I thought that I was going to be a drug addict for the rest of my life.

I had no hope for a better future. No hope for a better life. No hope for happiness.

As I cried in that empty room, I felt something. It was as if someone had just laid a hand on my back, and this tingly feeling came over me. The dog was lying down in the doorway to the room, and as I felt the presence of something other than myself enter the room, the dog jumped up on its hind legs and began to bark viciously at something above me. At the time, I had no idea what that presence was or why the dog was barking viciously.

I was beyond scared and ran out of the room. I began to tell my boyfriend what happened, and at first, he seemed to be in disbelief. I sat on the couch in the living room and unlocked my phone in hopes of getting some kind of service or access to an app, which was hard to do where we were located. When I unlocked my phone, the Jesus Calling app opened up without me tapping on it and, to my surprise, started loading. What was even more surprising was the fact that the app only had a five-day free trial period, and that trial period was long over. I hadn't paid to renew it.

That day, the devotional that Sara Young had written was directly from God to me. It was as if God was right there in that room, speaking directly to me, telling me that everything was going to be okay, that He was coming soon, and for me to hold on just a little longer. Tears streamed down my face as I started to read out loud to my boyfriend.

My boyfriend just stared at me as I read it to him. Then he said, "Rachel, don't you see? God has His hand on your life. There is a calling on your life."

At the time, I thought he was crazy. How could a severe drug addict be called by God? How am I going to do anything of any good for anyone? I couldn't even figure out how to clean myself up long enough, let alone help someone else.

This is just one of many times that the Lord mightily and supernaturally started speaking to me.

My hope in sharing this story is to reach people who were where I was – lost, alone, broken, and hopeless. To help people see that there is hope for a better future. There is a key to true happiness and someone that can help you achieve it.

The answer is God.

This book shares my journey on the road from death to victory, from the years before addiction when I was at my lowest through when God brought me out of it and beyond. I hope that you will be encouraged by my experience and that you will find healing, restoration, and deliverance yourself.

My prayer for you as you turn the page is that your hope will be restored and that your life will be transformed.

CHAPTER 1

Stealing My Innocence

I grew up with two loving parents, and from what my parents tell me, I had a pretty good childhood.

Psychologists say that when you go through something traumatic, your brain tends to stop maturing, which causes memory loss. I believe that is what happened to me. I don't remember much from my childhood, as if I started suppressing my emotions and my memories early on to the point of no return.

My parents did the best they knew how. They even raised us in church for most of my childhood. When I was five, my little brother was born with severe asthma. He cried a lot, and he clung to my mom, and it caused extra stress on my parents. I remember spending many nights at my grandma's because my parents needed a break.

This was when they started fighting, and as the fighting worsened, our church attendance declined. It got to a point where they were taking us and dropping us off at church, but they weren't attending themselves. I remember sitting in the church parking lot crying, begging my dad not to make me go into the church because the girls were mean to me. They made fun of me and were just cruel, and I started comparing myself to them. I was only eleven years old, looking at other girls thinking, *I'm not as pretty as her. I'm not as skinny as her. I'm not as outgoing as she is.*

Not only was I made fun of at church, but I was also made fun of at school too. People made fun of my last name, among many other things, but in my head, they might as well been making fun of my weight and my looks – or so the lies in my head told me. Those voices in my head were so strong and loud it felt like they were coming from actual people.

I realize now this was straight from the enemy. He was trying to stop me from accepting the call on my life by putting me in a constant cycle of comparison.

I'm not the only one either.

Despite what the media tells us, God did not make us all super skinny with blonde hair and blue eyes. God made us all differently. When He made each of us, He said He did a good job. Song of Solomon 4:7 says, "You are altogether beautiful, my darling; there is no flaw in you." This is what God said when He created you and me. He formed you in your mother's womb (Psalm 139:13). When He created you, He had your whole life planned out, and His plans for you are good. Jeremiah 29:11 says, "For I know the plans I have for you," declares the LORD, "plans to prosper you and not to harm you, plans to give you hope and a future."

God didn't create us to be rejected or made fun of; He created us with passion and purpose.

When we are rejected or made fun of, those lies get planted deeply and take root in our hearts. If we are not careful, they will take up a permanent space there, which will cause us to react to life's circumstances out of a place of hurt instead of a place of love. When we experience rejection and hurt, we have to take it to our Father God and ask Him to heal the hurt. We can ask Him to encourage us and show us the lie we are believing, and then to show us the truth to combat the lie.

We have to allow God to be everything to us. Otherwise, we will constantly be looking for love through all the things the world has to offer.

You may be finding yourself in a place like I did. I was so desperate to fit in that I was willing to do whatever it took to do so, which was not a good place to be. I was trying to fill the void I had in my heart with all the wrong things. I wanted to be a part of the cool crowd. I was craving attention. I desperately wanted to feel loved and needed. Looking back, I know my parents loved me, but for some reason, I wasn't feeling it. I looked in all the wrong places and was willing to do just about anything to get it.

When I turned twelve, we got a new neighbor. There were a couple of us neighborhood kids that would sit on his front porch and hang out with him. He would make us cookies and brownies, and we would just hang out.

We just thought he was our friend.

At the time, I was so naive that I didn't see how

this was wrong on many levels. I've blocked out many memories from those days, but what I can remember is some of the things our neighbor would say to me. He was always commenting on how pretty I was. He would say something like, "Your parents are just stupid for not allowing you to smoke and drink. If I were your dad, I would let you do anything you wanted to do." He filled my head with all kinds of lies, telling me that if I could ever find a way to sneak out one night, I could stay with him, and he would let me do whatever I wanted to do. He let me borrow movies I shouldn't be watching and made me and the other neighborhood girls business cards; we thought we were so cool.

He gained our trust by showering us with gifts and attention.

This was when my parents started to catch on. My mom had a bad feeling that something wasn't right, so she wouldn't let me go into his house, which made me so mad because the other girls did. Looking back on it, I'm glad she didn't. My parents eventually tapped our phone, so they could find out what was going on, not necessarily with our neighbor, but just in general. At this time, I was starting to rebel. They just knew something was going on with me but weren't sure what it was. To their surprise, they heard the conversations I was having with our neighbor. Like I said, I don't remember all the details, but from what my parents have told me, he said many perverted things to me and was inappropriate.

Once my parents heard these conversations, they confronted one of the other girls involved and me. As we sat on the couch, and they presented all this information to us, I got very angry. How dare they accuse my friend of such horrible things? They were telling us they were going to call the police on him, and I just couldn't understand why.

In the meantime, my parents called the police. I remember when the police showed up at our house, wanting to know the whole story and asking us to write out statements. I was so scared and confused.

For the next few months, we had to live like prisoners in our own home, trying to avoid him, while the police conducted an investigation. From the outside, nothing seemed to be happening. My parents were getting discouraged, thinking that nothing was going to come out of this. They decided to call a local church for some help. The pastor welcomed them in with open arms and got the ball rolling. The pastor got them in contact with the district attorney, and from that moment on, things just started happening. God was completely in this, and it was obvious. The police ended up getting a warrant to search his house, and what they found was appalling. They came out with half a truck bed full of child pornography along with drugs they had found in the attic. That was the day they took him into custody.

The trial process began. We were brought into the police department to give our statements again, and they questioned us. The police told my parents that our neighbor said he was ready to take it to the next level.

What would that have looked like?

Did he think that we would willingly do what he wanted us to do?

What if we would have said no?

Would he have forced us to do things anyway?

Honestly, I don't want to know, and I am so thankful that the Lord stepped in and stopped it from getting any worse.

One in every six women has experienced some form of sexual abuse. That statistic is awful to think about, but it is sadly true. I know many of you who are reading this have had much worse happen to you than I did, and for that, I am so very sorry. I'm sure you're searching for answers, wondering why God didn't protect you from it, or wondering what you did to deserve it. Here's the thing, you did nothing to deserve that kind of treatment. In fact, you should have never been put in that situation.

However, we live in a fallen world.

When Adam and Eve sinned in the garden, sin entered the world. In His infinite love for us, God gave us free will. People have the choice to do what they want when they want, and God cannot stop them from doing it, again, because of free will. This is why we have things like rape, theft, drug abuse, divorce, adultery, etc.

Most of the time, people are a byproduct of things they experienced in their own lives. Now, don't get me wrong; I am not giving an excuse for why people do what they do. What I am saying is that you are going to have to forgive them for what they have done to you. Forgiveness isn't saying what the person did to you was okay. Forgiveness simply heals your soul and frees you up to have a relationship with God. Sometimes it helps to think of the person who hurt you as being hurt themselves and not knowing any better. I know this is going to be hard for you, but holding on to the unforgiveness towards them is only going to hurt you more. This unforgiveness will turn into bitterness and resentment and will spill over into the rest of your life. (See the end of this chapter for a step by step guide on forgiveness.)

The trial eventually ended, and our neighbor was offered a plea bargain. He wasn't willing to take it at first, which would have meant us girls had to testify. I was so nervous as we all sat in this room waiting to see what his decision would be. I didn't want to get up in front of a room full of people with him sitting in front of me, telling them what he did to me.

As I was replaying all kinds of moments in my head, I can remember looking up and seeing our attorney enter the room and gather the parents together. As they talked, I could tell the news wasn't good. The parents walked over to us and began to tell us that he wasn't willing to take the plea bargain, and we were going to have to testify. All three of us immediately began to cry.

As our attorney ushered us into the courtroom, I could see him at the front of the room in handcuffs. He was in an orange jumpsuit with the slip-on shoes they give them. I can still remember the rage on his face. He turned around and took one look at us girls crying and leaned over to his attorney and whispered something to him. His attorney stood up and said that they would agree to take the plea bargain.

11

We were so relieved and yet, traumatized at the same time.

He got fifteen years, charged with several counts of lewd molestation, possession of child pornography, and possession of a controlled substance.

> "The thief comes only to steal, kill, and destroy; I have come that they may have life and have it to the full."
>
> John 10:10 (NIV)

I was too young to understand or to process what happened. I didn't know how to deal with the emotions I was feeling. I still didn't understand why what he did was wrong. What he did, though, prompted sexual curiosity and led me to do things like lose my virginity at fourteen, which I don't think I would have started doing at that age had I not been abused.

Finally, years later, I have gone through the healing process, and I now see that what he did was wrong. I now see that what he did led me down the wrong path. God took me through several different steps during the healing process. I had to go back and remember the events that took place, and as I did, it was as if He was going behind me with a Magic Eraser and erasing each one so that it wouldn't haunt me.

Then, God led me to pray for that man. At first, it was something I definitely didn't want to do. I felt like he stole my innocence. I felt like it was his fault that I went down the path I went down. However, I couldn't shake the fact that I kept hearing God tell me to pray for him.

So, it started like this. I would reluctantly say, "God, please bless _____." After a while, I was able to pray, "Lord, please bless _____ and please forgive him for what he did to me." Then it got even better, and I was able to forgive him completely. Once I forgave him for the things he did to me, it felt like a weight had been lifted off my shoulders, and I was able to start praying for his salvation.

I heard a story one time of a girl who was sexually abused by a family member. Later in her adolescent years, she was thinking back about that event, asking God where He was at that moment and why He didn't protect her. What she saw was a beautiful representation of our Father God. She saw herself lying there with her offender on top of her. Next to her, lying on the floor was Jesus. In the vision, she saw herself crying, and next to her, Jesus was crying too. Jesus was also hurting because she was being hurt, but because of free will on the offenders' part, there was nothing God could do to intervene.

God loves us and wants the very best for us; however, sometimes people's free will gets in the way and causes us pain. The good news is we don't have to live our life bound and oppressed by the pain of past hurts. We can come to God and ask Him to heal our hearts and erase the memories. He is a good Father, and He wants to take the pain you have been holding on to for years.

I also blamed God for allowing this to happen to me, and I had to forgive Him as well. It wasn't God's fault that this happened to me. We live in a fallen world, and I was merely a victim of someone who had fallen prey to the enemy. It sounds unfair, unjust, and sad, and it is, but I wouldn't change what I have been through for anything.

I want to add here that it is okay to be angry with God, but it is not okay to stay there. We are human, and He understands what it is like to be human and to have emotions because He came as a man in human form to this earth and experienced life as we do. He made us in His image, so He understands. When bad things happen to us, it is normal for us to immediately place blame and harbor ill feelings towards that person and others. For me, I had so much anger because I thought, *How could a good God that wants the best for me allow this to happen to me?* The answer is, He didn't allow it. Like I previously mentioned, we live in a fallen world. Sometimes people fall victim to another's sin, which means innocent people get hurt. It's hard to understand, but what I do know is, throughout it all, God never left my side.

I eventually went to God with all my anger. I expressed to Him why I was angry at Him and how I felt betrayed by Him for allowing me to go through all the hurt I experienced. In doing so, God showed me He never left my side through anything I had gone through. He took me through a process where He showed me where He was in every bad situation. Going through this process taught me that He loved me and wanted the best for me and that it was not His fault I went through the things I did. I no longer hold anger towards God, nor am I bitter or resentful for the situations I went through. Going through everything I went through has made me the person I am today.

God wants us to be honest with Him. Don't hold

on to feelings of bitterness and resentment toward Him until it negatively shapes the way you see people and the world around you. Let it out. Tell God how you feel. Get those thoughts and feelings out in the open so that you and God can start the healing process.

I hope you can one day look back on the event that changed your life forever and have the same attitude. We go through things, and although they hurt, they make us stronger and turn us into the people God has destined for us to be.

Keys to Finding Freedom:

If someone has sexually abused you, and you have not told anyone, please find someone to tell. It took me fourteen years to open up to someone and talk to them about it, but once I did, I received healing. You will too!

Do not listen to the lies. They may be telling you that if you tell someone, they will hurt you or your family. They are only threatening you so that they won't get caught. It will not end until you bring it to the light by telling someone.

My prayer for you is that you will be brave enough to tell someone, even if the abuse has stopped. It only hurts you more by keeping it in and keeping it secret.

"For everything that is hidden or secret will eventually be brought to light and made plain to all."

Luke 8:17

15

Here are some steps that may help you in the healing process:

1. Ask the Lord to reveal areas from your past that need to be healed.
2. Ask Him what your part is in it. Do you need to forgive someone? Confront someone? Tell someone?
3. Ask God to show you where He was when the event took place.
4. Forgive the person who hurt you.
5. Pray for the person who hurt you.

I believe if you follow these steps, God will release His healing upon you. Know that I am praying for you during this time, that God will make Himself known in your heart and your life, and that you will be released from the oppression you have been carrying from the past hurt.

Pray this prayer with me:

Lord, I pray that You would bring this situation to light. Come in and fill up all the dark places I have held back from You. Give me the courage to do what needs to be done. Help me see that it was not my fault. Help me to forgive the person who hurt me. Help me to see myself the way you see me. Allow the shame and guilt I have carried to fall off of me. Bring back my smile, Lord, and remove the anger from my life. I choose to forgive _____ for hurting me. And I will choose to pray blessings on their life instead of holding on to the unforgiveness.

In Jesus' name,
Amen.

CHAPTER 2

Trying to Fit In

There are two kingdoms in this world, one of light and one of darkness. God is the ruler of the kingdom of light, and Satan is the ruler of the kingdom of darkness. Satan is alive and very real. Take a look around you at all the negative you see in this world; this is a product of the enemy's efforts.

God has called us to live pure lives. According to Galatians 5:22, our lives should be full of the fruit of the spirit. "But the fruit of the Spirit is love, joy, peace, forbearance, kindness, goodness, faithfulness." Satan wants the opposite for us and is willing to do anything to make us fail.

My parents tried to raise me in church, and until about the age of twelve, I stayed. On October 17, 1999, I gave my life to Christ. I was standing in the back of the church with my family. As the pastor gave an altar call, I felt the Lord's presence so strongly that I left my seat and walked to the front.

I accepted Jesus into my heart that day. A year later is when I was molested by my next-door neighbor.

It's evident to me now that that was Satan's first attempt at trying to stop me and the calling that God had placed on my life. Instead of seeking God in the aftermath as I should have, I did the very opposite. I became so curious about all the wrong things. I completely turned my back on God during this time and started to seek out what the world had to offer instead.

By the time I hit my teens, I was a mess. I had so much anger built up and wasn't even sure why I was angry or where it had come from. I was very rebellious and regularly fought with my parents. Simply put, I wanted to do what I wanted, when I wanted, and I didn't care what anyone had to say about it.

Depression followed the rebellion, and I started looking for happiness in all the wrong places. Specifically, in the "in-crowd."

I wanted so desperately to fit in with the cool crowd that I was willing to do whatever it took, including stealing from department stores. The people I wanted to fit in with wanted me to steal, and I wanted to be cool. So, I thought if I did it, I was "in." I rejected a couple of genuinely good friends and went all in to try to win the approval of the crowd. But they were only using me.

Once the popular crowd realized they didn't need

me anymore, I realized I had no friends, was alone again, and was still depressed.

During middle school, I became friends with a girl for a short time until she started experiencing emotional distress. During the time that we were friends, she taught me how to cut myself as well as how to attract the attention I was seeking by exhibiting unhealthy behavior. It seemed harmless at first, just something to take the edge off the pain. The first time I cut, I remember thinking, *This hurts, but not as bad as I am hurting inside.* But in reality, it was making me feel just as bad on the outside as I did on the inside.

Before I started writing this book, I reread my diaries to help me remember important details that I may have blocked out. That's where I read this entry.

October 20th, 2003

"I've been so depressed lately! I just feel like I don't belong anywhere anymore. I've told people this, but no one seems to understand or listen for that matter. I don't feel like killing myself anymore, but I have cut myself again. I really don't know if this is for attention or if I'm so depressed, I'm really doing it. I just don't see things for the way they are anymore. I just want to be happy again."

In the beginning, it was a cry for help, a call for attention.

At first, I tried to hide it, but someone eventually found out and told the counselor at school who called my parents. When my parents found out, they were so mad. They didn't understand what was so bad that I would want to take my own life.

Honestly, I didn't want to kill myself; I just wanted something to take the pain away. My mom picked me up early from school that day, and my dad took off work early. I sat on the couch in tears as my dad told me if I wanted to kill myself that I needed to cut up and down, not side-to-side. I thought they were mad, but in reality, they were horrified to think I would kill myself and not be in their life. The truth was I was broken inside, and I could feel myself trying to yell for help, but nothing came out. They didn't understand. I was only trying to cope with how I was feeling inside, and this was the only way I knew how.

If only they knew I was hurting.

If only they knew I felt like an outcast.

If only they knew I felt lost and alone.

But how were they to know when I didn't even know myself?

This was the first of many cries for help. My parents sent me to three different therapists, but they couldn't help me. What I was dealing with was far more complicated, and the fact that I couldn't put it into words didn't help much. I tried, but I couldn't connect or open up to them. I was so young, I didn't understand what was going on, why I was feeling the way I was feeling, or why I was doing the things that I was doing.

So, it continued.

I thought that cutting was a new thing when I did it over ten years ago. However, I was reading in 1 Kings the other day and came across this verse:

> "So, they shouted louder, and following their normal custom, they cut themselves with knives and swords until the blood gushed out."

1 Kings 18:28

Cutting isn't new. This is something people dealt with even back in the Bible days because the enemy's strategy hasn't changed. His only weapon is to deceive. If he can make you think your life is bad enough, then he can put thoughts into your mind to prompt you to end it. That is a lie!

When the thoughts manifest, you probably hear things like this.

"I am not good enough."

"No one likes me."

"I am not pretty enough."

"I am not skinny enough."

What you choose to do with those thoughts will make or break your future actions. Instead of dwelling on the negative thoughts, you have to take them captive and cast them down. What does that look like? When a negative thought comes into your mind, you can either continue to think about it all day, or you can say, "No, that thought is not true of me, and I choose not to believe it."

Now, I know that sometimes we do all we know to do. We speak the scriptures over ourselves, we cast down the wrong thoughts, and we pray and believe. We do all the things, and yet we still see no improvement. I'm not acting like I have all the answers because I don't. I am still walking this thing out just like you are. However, I do know that sometimes when praying and fasting and believing isn't working, it is because we have deep issues from our past that need to be ripped out and healed at the deepest level.

If this is something you are struggling with, it might be a good idea to ask God to reveal areas where you still need healing. After he shows you what it is, ask him what you need to do to move on from it and be healed.

Do you need to forgive yourself?

Forgive someone else?

Throw something away?

Change your thoughts?

Change your actions?

No matter the issue, God is the answer. And although it may feel like you are in the darkest hole you have ever been in with no way out, if you seek after God, He will save you.

Deuteronomy 4:29-31 says, "But if from there you will seek the LORD your God, you will find Him if you seek Him with all your heart and with all your soul. When you are in distress, and all these things have happened to you, then in later days you will return to the Lord your God and obey him. For the

TRYING TO FIT IN

Lord your God is a merciful God; he will not
abandon or destroy you or forget the covenant with your ancestors, which he confirmed
to them by oath." (NIV)

Your life is worth so much more than you know.
You were made for a reason with a purpose to accom-
plish. "For I know the plans I have for you," declares
the LORD, "plans to prosper you and not to harm you,
plans to give you hope and a future." Jeremiah 29:11
(NIV) Before God even created you, He knew who
you would be and what you would do. He knew who
you would become. He knew what mistakes you would
make and how your life would end. We are all here for
a reason. The question is, are you willing to do what it
takes to figure out what the Lord has destined you to
be?

If this is something you're struggling with, I want
to encourage you to seek out someone you can open
up to about how you are feeling and what's going on.
Keeping this bottled up inside of you will only make it
worse. I consider it a blessing that someone told on me.
It saved my life. It brought it to my parent's attention,
and although it wasn't handled well, it still brought the
situation to light instead of keeping it a secret. Secrets
will only keep you sick.

Mark 4:22 says, "For everything that is hidden will eventually be brought into the open,
and every secret will be brought to light."

I also want to tell you not to be ashamed of your scars. Your scars are truly beautiful. They are a reminder that God does exist and that He loves you enough to save your life. God has the ultimate scars on His body because He loved you so much that He was willing to pay the price for all sin so that you could live a life of freedom. So, reach out to someone and receive your freedom.

Lord, I pray right now for the person reading this book. I pray that You would open their heart to receive Your love. I pray that You would shine down on them right now with Your everlasting love and forgiveness. I thank You that You are healing their hearts right now from hurtful words, physical abuse, and even sexual abuse. Father, I thank You that You are changing their perspective on life right now. Bring them the peace that surpasses all understanding and unspeakable joy. Wrap Your arms of love around them and help them to feel Your presence right now.

In the name of Jesus,
Amen.

CHAPTER 3

Running Wild

During the situation with my next-door-neighbor, my parents and I had the opportunity to take a class that the courts offered to help me get ready for court. They separated my parents and me, taking me to view the courtroom to help ease my mind about the possibility of having to testify while they took my parents to a separate room and talked to them about abused children. That's where my parents first heard that after being molested, I would either be afraid of men or become very promiscuous. At the time, I didn't see myself as being promiscuous, but looking back on it, I very much was. I always had a boyfriend, along with two to three other guys on the side, sometimes my boyfriend's friends or brothers. I didn't know how to be alone.

It was like I was continually running from myself to anything that would show me a glimpse of love, if even only for a moment.

The guy-next-door used to tell me that my parents were just stupid and that they just didn't want me to have any fun. He would say that if I were able to stay the night with him, he would let me do whatever I wanted to do. Although I was raised right, his words played in the back of my head, fueling my rebellion even more. I was angry, lost, hurting, and confused. I didn't know what a good marriage looked like, or even a healthy relationship.

My curiosity led me to an online relationship. Well before the generation of webcams and smartphones, we talked for months before we met in person or saw a picture of each other. The first time we met in person was at a youth group gathering at a church. At first, I was unsure, but the bond that we had created overpowered my uncertainty. It was only a matter of months before I decided I wanted to lose my virginity to him.

I had been taught that having sex before marriage was wrong, but I never understood why. No one ever explained that part to me. In the back of my mind, I was still playing my neighbor's words that my parents just didn't want me to have any fun. So, I did whatever I wanted, not caring about what would happen or what people would say.

When God created man and woman, he also created sex. He told Adam and Eve in the garden to be fruitful and multiply – to have sex and create a family – and God called it good. We have a hard time believing that sex is a good thing and that God created it because the enemy has come in and perverted it, making it seem shameful. But that's not how it was designed; instead, it was meant to be a gift within the walls of marriage – a covenant.

Whenever two people have sex – married or not – they form a covenant, or a bond, promise, agreement, or contract. As a result, when you sleep with someone, you are taking on all of their issues, and that person is taking on all of yours.

Have you ever wondered why you're all of a sudden struggling with extreme anger, insecurity, or anxiety more after sleeping with someone? You may think, "I never struggled with this before," and now, after sleeping with that person, you feel like a different person. The truth is sex is a powerful thing. It binds you and ties you to the person, physically, emotionally, and even spiritually. Having sex with a person is essentially like marrying them without the marriage ceremony. Every time you have sex with a person, you are accepting their issues, thoughts, and beliefs and taking them on as your own. This is called a soul tie. A soul tie is when two people have sex and become spiritually and physically linked together.

After sleeping with guys, I would become so possessive and obsessive, especially if they were cheating on me. I would start looking through their phones, showing up unannounced at their homes, and just acting completely crazy. For more in-depth information on this subject, see Pastor Mike Todd's sermon series called *Relationship Goals* from Transformation Church.

The night I lost my virginity, I lost a piece of myself I would never be able to get back.

I remember sitting on the bathroom floor of his house, sobbing uncontrollably. In the back of my mind, I knew that what I was doing was wrong, but I still didn't understand why it was wrong. From that moment forward, it was as if sexual acts were what made me feel loved and how I showed love.

I ran wild, just like the court told my parents I would. I was running after anything that would make me feel loved, which never lasted long.

I was with this guy for a little over a year. Throughout that year, I cheated on him many times. He was honestly a great guy and treated me better than any guy I've ever been with, but for whatever reason, I couldn't see that. I couldn't make myself love him the way he loved me. I wanted to, and I tried to, but I couldn't. I was broken, and sadly it wasn't his fault, but he fell victim to it.

You can't make someone love you or make yourself love someone else. Also, the harder you run after something to make you feel loved, the more you will see that nothing fills the hole in your heart like God can. God created us to be able to love and be loved. His greatest commandment is to love one another.

Matthew 22:37-39 says, "Love the Lord your God with all your heart and with all your soul and with all your mind. This is the first and greatest commandment. And the second is like it: 'Love your neighbor as yourself'" (NIV).

God created us for love; however, we must first love ourselves and love him before we can love anyone else. I'm sure you've heard the expression, "trying to fill the void in your heart." If you haven't, that's something people say when they see girls or even guys running after all the world has to offer.

That's what I did.

I'm sure some part of you is struggling with this as well. What do you run to? Drugs, cutting, food, men, friends, TV? When we are down and upset about how our day went, we turn to other things to drown out the pain. Until we make God our number one, we will continue to make wrong decisions.

So, what does that look like? When you have had a bad day, instead of coming home and getting a cupcake and turning on your favorite show, what about going to your room and spending time with God? Tell Him how your day went. Tell Him how it made you feel and ask Him what you need to do about the given situation. We must allow room in our lives for God to enter in and change things, or we will continue to run around banging our heads against the wall.

During the years I was with the guy I lost my virginity to, I started having guys sneak into my room; I was beyond boy crazy. I also began sneaking out and experimenting with alcohol and drugs, including marijuana and ecstasy. I was getting drunk at school in the bathrooms, taking pills at school, and getting so wasted that I couldn't remember the night before. There were many nights that I would blackout, waking up the next morning with no memory of the night before, or how I got back to my room.

I was continually looking for new ways to get high. Drinking made me blackout and very sick the next morning, so I started seeking out something better. By the ninth grade, I had found pain pills, Adderall, and Xanax, and I was in love. When I couldn't find anything else, I would binge drink, and as a last resort, I would smoke weed. Weed made me paranoid, and I didn't like it, but it was better than being sober.

What started as an outlet to make friends quickly turned into something I had to have to function in my daily routines. After constantly consuming different substances, it takes a toll on your body to the point where you can't wake up without something. You can't get through your day without something.

And by fifteen, this is where I found myself.

No one knew the pain I was feeling inside. No one knew that I was crying out for help. No one knew because I didn't tell them, but I didn't know how to tell them. Honestly, I didn't even know myself at the time. High school is such a weird time in life to begin with. It is a time where you are supposed to be finding out who you are, yet for most, it's a time of insecurities and rejection. At least it was for me.

Keys to Finding Freedom:

Please hear me when I say I am in no way condoning this behavior and saying you should do this. I am merely sharing my story to show people who are going through the same things I did how dangerous and out of control this lifestyle truly is. I wish someone would have told me the repercussions my actions would have had before I made all the mistakes I did.

My prayer for you is that in reading my story, your eyes would be open to seeing things for how they are and not for how you want them to be. I know you may be thinking that drugs and sex are a path to forget or to feel loved and wanted, but the truth is all those feelings will only come flooding back in the morning, along with guilt and shame for your actions. Day after day, you will continue to do this with no permanent ending to your misery. The only way you will ever get past your hurts, mistakes, and problems is turning to the One that can wipe it all away.

God is up there waiting for you to turn to Him. He has never left your side. He loves you, regardless of the things you have done. He loves you, regardless of how many people you have slept with. He loves you, regardless of how many nights you don't remember. He loves you, regardless of how many people you have betrayed. He loves you, regardless of how many crimes you have committed. He loves you, regardless of the babies you have aborted. He loves you. He died for you. He died so that you may have life and have it to the fullest.

It says in John 10:10, "The thief comes only to steal and kill and destroy, but Jesus has come so that you may have life and have it to the full" (NIV). Running wild after the things of this world is the enemy's tactic to get you wrapped up in sin so that your focus will be shifted from God. When that happens, you get so lost in what you're doing that you can't see the light. God is saying to you right now, "Step out of the darkness and come to the light. Let me guide you. Let me hold you. Let me love you."

Right now, I would like you to pray this prayer over yourself:

Father, I know that I am a sinner. I know that You died for me to rid me of the shame and guilt that I carry around. Help me to let go of the past. Help me to run after You with my whole heart. Help me to step out of the darkness and into the light. Help me to let go of the things that are hindering me. I choose to turn to You, God. I choose to love You and not the things of this world. I will run after You all the days of my life.

In Jesus' name,
Amen

If you are ready to break soul ties in your life from past partners, I have included a prayer below for you to pray. (for more teaching on soul ties, see resources in the back of the book.)

First, I want you to sit down and make a list of people, places, or things you need to break ties with. The thing about soul ties is it can honestly be anything. I had to break ties with drugs, food, sex, and even family members. Soul ties don't just happen because you have sex with someone. There are also emotional soul ties, as well. So, start by sitting down and asking the Lord to help you come up with a list of everyone or everything you need to break soul ties with. Then go through each one and pray this prayer.

Father God, thank You for Your delivering

and healing power. I thank You that I can come to You with these sins and lay them at Your feet, and not only will You forgive me, but You will heal me from the bondage. I confess right now that I _____ (names or details of the sin). Please forgive me for the sins I have committed against You. In the name of Jesus and through the powerful blood of Jesus Christ, I cut myself free from the ties that had me bound. I rebuke and renounce any evil spirits that may have tried to attach themselves to me or cause me harm. Father, please heal me of all past wounds and any hangs up in my spiritual walk with You that these sins have caused. Purify my mind and heart, Lord.

In Jesus' name, amen!

I truly believe if you go through this prayer with the soul ties, you will see and experience deeper love and relationship with our Father. For me, this step was one of the crucial steps I took through my healing that made all the difference.

CHAPTER 4

Way of Escape

On my fourteenth birthday, a friend introduced me to cocaine.

We told my mom that a friend of ours had injured himself in a motorcycle wreck, and we wanted to say hi to him. So, she drove us over there and sat in the car while we ran inside this guy's house to buy a sack. I walked into this house, and there were three guys there. On the table, I saw several lines along with piles of cocaine next to them. It was the most of any kind of drug I had ever seen. It honestly didn't even affect me as it would today. I was so young and naïve. I didn't realize how dangerous of a situation I was in.

That night, we snorted the lines in my room. This only piqued my interest in what else was out there for me to do. During this time, I would take just about anything I came across, including taking ecstasy at school and eventually stealing my dad's Klonopin. I started watching the show *Intervention*, which is a documentary on drug addict's lives. It shows them go through their everyday lives, and in the end, they have a surprise intervention with their family. I would watch this show all the time, and it again only piqued my interest in drugs more.

I started dating a guy named Ryder, who ran around with a bunch of people who did ecstasy. I loved it from the first try. From that moment forward, I was seeking that "first time feeling" again and never succeeded. I did ecstasy more times than I can count. Each time was horrible. I ended up freaking out. I wouldn't want anyone to touch me or even be around me. I hated the way it made me feel, but for some reason, I kept getting talked into doing it one more time. People would say, "Oh, you just weren't with the right people, or you didn't have the right atmosphere, or you didn't have the right lighting." That just wasn't the case, but each time I got talked into it, and it only led to another bad experience. What I later learned is my body doesn't process things correctly. I have had this problem my whole life with medicines and drugs alike - they wouldn't work the way they were supposed to.

Ryder eventually started selling ecstasy to make a profit, which introduced me to selling drugs. On the night that he graduated high school, we got a hotel room and took some Klonopin. I don't remember anything from that night; however, the next morning, I was still feeling the effects of the pills and had to drive to his mom's house. I also had to go pick up my brother and drop him off at my grandma's house. After dropping my brother off at my grandma's house, Ryder's mom had called me to find out where I was, and I told her I was only two miles up the road. I went to hang up my phone and must have looked down. The next thing I knew, I was sliding off the road into a huge pothole. I overcompensated and spun around into the next lane. I don't remember much after that. I was told that a truck came up behind me and hit me, pushing me into a field.

When I came to, I was on a stretcher being put into an ambulance. I can remember feeling my chin gushing blood, and honestly, my thought was, *Oh no, I am going to get blood all over my shirt.* Then I felt around in my mouth and realized I was missing a tooth. I must have been in and out of consciousness because the next thing I remember is being in the hospital and the nurses making me move over to a different bed so that they could x-ray my back and make sure there was no permanent damage. The whole thing was crazy. My mom said that the firefighters on the scene were walking out into the field to get all of my belongings because most of my stuff was catapulted far out into the field.

I got a ticket for being left of center and for not wearing a seat belt. When I got out of the hospital, we went to the impound lot to look at my car. The trunk was smashed up against the front seat. It was a miracle I was alive. The only things I walked away with were twelve stitches in my chin and a broken tooth.

You can't tell me there isn't a God.

I should have died in that wreck, but I didn't because my life was destined for greatness, and so is yours.

I was prescribed pain pills for the pain from the wreck. This is what started my addiction to them. This was finally a drug that I could take that wouldn't make me feel bad the next day. I enjoyed doing them. They made me feel great and didn't seem to have any side effects, at least at first. I eventually found a doctor that prescribed me all kinds of pain pills and Adderall. This only led me down another path of addiction. It got to where I couldn't get the prescriptions to last as long as they were supposed to, which led me to the streets to find more. I couldn't even make it from paycheck to paycheck anymore. I was borrowing money from co-workers just to support my habit. I would get sick for days when I would go without the pills causing me to call into work all the time. My body was literally shutting down, but I didn't even realize that it was because of the pills I was taking. I went to all kinds of doctors and had all sorts of tests ran to find out what was wrong with me, when it was just the pills messing up my body.

By this time, I had found out that Ryder was cheating on me with so many people that I lost count. He was even cheating on me with my friends. Not only was it with girls, but come to find out, it was with guys too. I was devastated. I stopped eating for a while but kept taking excessive amounts of pills. You can see why my body was shutting down. I was in such a deep state of depression that I didn't want to get out of bed. I started rapidly losing weight, which only made things worse.

During this time, my parents told my brother and I that they were going to get a divorce. This rocked my world even more.

That night I was in my room, and I heard my parents yell for my brother and me to come to the living room. It was obvious they were upset about something. I thought to myself, *Oh no, what have they caught me doing now?* This happened quite often. They had found alcohol in water bottles in my room before, and they had seen notes people had written to me talking about stuff I shouldn't be doing. So, I thought I was in trouble; I couldn't have been more wrong. My mom proceeded to tell me that they would no longer be living together. That they were going to get a divorce.

I started bawling and screaming at my mom while my dad held me. I felt like it was all her fault. My brother was crying too, but he clung to my mom. Afterward, my brother and I went to my room and laid on my bed. This was the night we finally became close. The next morning, I was a wreck. I went to school without makeup on and in sweat pants. Teachers tried getting on to me for not doing work, and I was hateful to them. One got on to me, and I hatefully said my parents are getting divorced. She left me alone after that.

The next few months were hard. My dad still stayed with us and moved into my brother's room with him while they looked for a house for him to buy. I started drinking more during this time, and it just continued to get out of control. By this time, Ryder had moved out into his own place, and he had parties all the time. Girls at school were telling me they were at his parties and how they saw him with other girls. I was going crazy. I became that crazy girlfriend. I would show up at his place, yelling and cussing at him. I would lose all control and blackout and just start punching him; sometimes, I even punched holes in his walls. I had turned into a person I didn't even recognize anymore.

I had so much anger and felt like I didn't deserve to be treated right.

I was severely depressed. I skipped school a lot during this time, along with dabbling in other drugs.

I was on a constant chase for the next best thing.

At one point, I started cheating on Ryder too, with whomever I thought would hurt him worse. This included the people closest to him. I wanted to inflict as much pain as possible on him because, in my eyes, nothing I could ever do to him would amount to all the pain and heartache he had caused me. I just kept going down a road that was only hurting me more. I ignored all the warning signs and continued full force ahead.

I had so much anger at this point in life and didn't know how to properly release it. I would get so angry with Ryder that I would punch him in the face on multiple occasions. My mom and I would fight a lot too, and a couple of times, it got physical. At the time, I didn't know I could go to God with my problems. I didn't think I could talk to God about what was going on and ask him for help. I felt alone and lost. I felt like no one cared, and I was in constant pain.

What I didn't know then is that God is available all the time to talk. In John 14:16-18, we see that Father God sent his Holy Spirit for our benefit. It says, "And I will ask the Father, and he will give you another advocate to help you and be with you forever – the Spirit of truth. The world cannot accept him because it neither sees him nor knows him. But you know him, for he lives with you and will be in you. I will not leave you as orphans; I will come to you."

The Holy Spirit is with us all day every day. We

can just start talking and know that he is listening. John 14:26 says, "But the Helper (Comforter, Advocate, Intercessor-Counselor, Strengthener, Standby), the Holy Spirit, whom the Father will send in My name [in My place, to represent Me and act on My behalf], He will teach you all things. And He will help you remember everything that I have told you." The Holy Spirit was sent to help us, guide us, direct us, love on us, comfort us, and listen to us. He is there 24/7 for our benefit. It is important to remember that when we are going through hard times. It is also essential to find an outlet to channel our pain and anger. I always wished I would've found a sport, an instrument, or some form of art to pour myself into instead of turning to drugs. Find something you like to do and let that be your outlet.

Keys to Finding Freedom:

I wish I would've known then what I know now. It would have saved me so much hurt. When you get lost in it, you can't see what's right in front of you. I hope that if you are reading this and you are going through the same things as I was that this would be a warning sign to you to stop. That you will see it and make a decision to stop. It isn't going to get any better or any easier. In fact, it will only get worse. You will only cry more and hurt more. It says in the Bible that sin is only pleasurable for a season. That couldn't be truer. As you continue to read this book, you will see it only got worse for me, and the same will be true for you if you don't stop now. You may think that you've got this, that you can handle this, and it will get better. But the truth is, honey, only God can help you get out of this mess.

Please trust me on this. Run to God, and let Him help you. If you are ready to make a change and want to turn from your ways, here's a prayer you can pray.

Lord Jesus, I love You. I thank You for dying on the cross for me to pay for my sinful actions. Right now, Lord, I am choosing to make a change in my life for the better. I am admitting fault and admitting my weakness for making bad decisions. I am asking You to help me stand against the temptations of this world. Bring good, godly people into my life that will help build me up and not tear me down. Help me to find the things of this world repulsive. Forgive me for the things that I have done wrong. I forgive myself for the things that I have done wrong. I forgive all people who have hurt me. I choose to turn to You to find my self-worth. Help me to see myself the way You see me, Father. Show me my purpose on this earth and help me to walk in it. Lord, thank You for loving me even when it seemed that no one else was.

In Jesus' name,
Amen.

When I went to treatment, several steps helped in my deliverance, freedom, and healing. The first thing that had to be done was committing my life to Christ. I had to repent for my sins and ask Him to come into my life. I had to make a change. This is just one of many steps I will touch on throughout this book. However, if you are ready to make that change too, here is a prayer you can pray:

> Father God, I am sorry for all the sins I have committed. I am sorry for turning my back on You. Please forgive me for my past actions. I know that You are real and that You died on the cross for me. Please come into my life as Lord and Savior, and change me, mold me, make me into the person You have called me to be.
>
> In Jesus' name,
> Amen!

CHAPTER 5

Continuing the Cycle

Nothing ever seemed to be good enough. I was always searching for something better, for the next best thing. This led me down even darker paths. I went through stages when I was younger where I started sneaking out, and my parents found out about it. When they confronted me about it, my dad said, "What am I going to have to do, board up your window?" I was so defiant, I yelled, "GO FOR IT!" I was doing nothing but getting into trouble anyway. I had already lost my virginity at that point and was sneaking out to meet other guys and go party.

By the time my parents took the board off my window, I had friends who had cars. I was so sneaky and manipulative; I was always getting by with something. I had many moments where I had gotten myself into dangerous situations. I was at a party one night, and the girl that I went with ended up getting in a car with another guy. These guys were much older than us. I didn't know any of them. I thought I heard some of them talking about getting us alone. When she left me, I was terrified. I tried to stop her, but she wouldn't listen to me. Yet again, it was God who got me out of that situation. I was able to call some of my friends, and they came and picked us up.

One night, my boyfriend at the time and I went to the county fair here in Tulsa. As we were leaving, he decided to roll up a joint for us to smoke on the way home. As he lit it up, traffic got stopped by a police officer allowing pedestrians to walk across the crosswalk. Of course, he smelled marijuana. He followed it straight to our car and yelled for us to pull over onto the grass. I can remember shaking because I was so scared. They pulled us out of the vehicle. The police officers ended up making me call my dad because I was underage, and they ended up letting my boyfriend call a friend since he was overage. Yet again, this was God's grace - his crazy, unmerited favor and protection that I didn't deserve - in my life. They could have arrested us, but they honestly didn't have time to deal with us since they were supposed to be directing traffic for the fair.

The relationship I had with this guy was violent and manipulative. For the first six months, he made me feel important, loved, and wanted. He made me feel like I was the only one he ever loved this way and that I mattered to him. After a while, he became a completely different person. It was as if he sucked me in, and then once he had me, he could do whatever he wanted to me. I allowed him to cheat on me continuously. Every time I would find out about another girl, we would fight, and I would physically hit him because I would get so angry. I had so much anger bottled up inside of me that when it came out, it was violent. He helped fuel that fire. I also said that he made me crazy, that he made me into the person that I had become. Granted, it didn't help, but I had already had so many problems and issues that I hadn't dealt with that this was just a result of all that.

This went on for two years and only got worse. I was a wreck. I wasn't eating, I was skipping school regularly, and my drinking got heavier. I started to become even more promiscuous. All of my acts of rebellion never helped; it honestly only made me feel worse about myself and my situation. I continued to find myself in relationship after relationship, and each one was even worse than the one before. Eventually, the current boyfriend I was with took me over to one of his friends' houses, and he introduced me to my next boyfriend, Oliver.

I couldn't be single and alone. I didn't know how to be.

I was beginning to think that these types of relationships were the norm, but I am here to tell you that being hit, yelled at, cussed out, or abused in any way is not real love. It is not the way God has called relationships to be. Hurting people hurt people, and that is a fact. That is the reason why I kept attracting guys who only hurt me. You have to get yourself right before you can bring someone into your life.

The previous boyfriend ended up moving to another state for a few months, and during that time, I continued to go over to Oliver's apartment. In a matter of a few days, we ended up together. One of the first nights we spent together, we had a couple of my friends come over, and we took what they call Triple C's, which is an over-the-counter cough and cold medicine called Coricidin. At first, I can remember lying on the ground and saying that I saw footballs with flames. I was happy and laughing, then the next minute I was throwing up, and everything was spinning. I thought I was going to lose my life that night, but Oliver stayed by my side all night long. He never left me. He barely knew me, and he held my hair for me when I threw up, he wiped my face for me and sat in the bathroom with me for hours. He was like the perfect gentlemen all night. He took me upstairs, put me in bed, and just laid there all night with me to make sure I was okay while the party continued downstairs.

That was the night I fell in love with him.

I had never been taken care of like that and was once again finding love in the wrong place. We continued our drug habits together. We rolled together, drank together, and smoked weed together. He only had a couple more weeks left on his lease for that apartment, and for the next two weeks, it was party central at his house. Before I was dating Oliver and was still with the previous guy, Oliver would have friends come over, and they would stay upstairs in his bedroom for hours. I never understood why. I finally figured out they were doing a drug called meth. I had never heard of it before. It was first described to me as an "upper." I was told there were no bad side effects to it, temporary or long term, and that people couldn't tell you were on anything. However, for some reason, I still had a bit of a fear about it.

When we got together, I told him that I would only be with him if he promised never to do that stuff again because I would see him come home from long nights at the casino acting weird and being mean. I didn't want any part of that. He agreed he wouldn't do it anymore, and we became an item. One of the last days at his apartment, two people came over because they needed somewhere to smoke (meth). He allowed them to smoke and asked me if he could please smoke with them. It didn't look bad, they didn't act funny, they didn't get angry, and I really couldn't see any harm in it. They even assured me there were no bad side effects to it. I told him I would only allow him to do it if he let me do it too, and he agreed. Little did I know this would be the start to something even bigger.

Keys to Finding Freedom:

Every bad decision I ever made was because of the influence of someone else I was around. I would have never gone and sought out meth on my own. That's why it is so important that you surround yourself with people you want to be like. Surround yourself with good, godly people because as much as you want to change the person you're with, they will eventually drag you down to where they are.

I heard it put this way. Imagine that you are standing up on top of a chair, and the person you are in a relationship with is standing on the ground. As much as you want to pull them up with you on to the chair, they are going to win at pulling you down with them.

It is so important to guard your heart and your mind. This means if there is someone in your life right now that is negative all the time or stuck in addiction, and you are trying to better yourself, you are going to have to cut them out.

Your freedom is at stake.

Your life depends on it.

It may be hard right now, but it will be even harder in the end if you hang on. When I came home from Mercy, I had to cut all ties with all the people from my past. It was hard, and it hurt my heart. But had I not done that, I could have fallen right back into the same patterns and routines. I have seen it happen too many times. People go back to the same environments and fall right back into the same situations and habits.

Is there something that God is asking you to let go of? He is a gentleman; He will not force you to let go of something. Instead, He will ask you to let go of it. However, please know that He would not be asking you to let go of something if it wasn't in your best interest. Most of the time, if we would just let go of what God is asking us to let go of, He has something even better waiting for us on the other side.

Ask yourself these questions:

1. Is it worth holding on to?
2. Why do I not want to let _____ go?
3. What is it fulfilling within me?
4. Can God take over that fulfillment in that area in my life?
5. What would life be like if I gave up _____ and if I didn't give it up?

Get honest with yourself. Seek out the answers to these questions. It could be regarding addiction or a person, or it could be negativity, insecurity, cussing, wrong thought patterns. Honestly, God loves you and wants the very best for you. He can see the harmful patterns you are stuck in. If He is asking you to let go of something, know that it is for your benefit. It can completely change your life. Give it a try!

CHAPTER 6

Addicted to Love

They say that when you try meth, you are hooked from the first hit. I never thought that could be true, nor did I think that would happen to me.

The first time I tried meth was in a boyfriend's apartment. It was about three in the afternoon. From the first moment the smoke hit my lungs, I was in love. I felt this tingling sensation come over my body, and I was more awake than I had ever been in my life. I had all kinds of energy. I was ready to get up and clean the entire apartment with just a toothbrush. I wondered how I had never heard of this stuff before. I found something that I loved even more than pain pills. Was this real? I wanted this feeling to last forever.

That night I went to my first college class. It was a whole new world. I retained everything I heard the teacher say, all the while drawing a checkerboard on my notebook paper. I felt alive for the first time in my life.

I felt untouchable, unbreakable, and unshakeable. I wondered if anyone could tell I was on something, but really, I didn't care. I felt so good. I felt invisible. Nothing in that moment mattered except smoking again. I was starting to come down by the end of the class, so I texted my boyfriend to ask if he could get some more, but he couldn't. So, we decided to get ecstasy that night instead.

It was a constant chase. I was always looking for something to get me high.

I don't tell you all of this so you can become curious and want to try it yourself. Yes, at first, it is glorious, but I haven't gotten to the downfall yet. Although I felt like I was on top of the world, it didn't take long before everything came crashing down.

In the Bible, it clearly says that sin is only pleasurable for a season (Hebrews 11:25). Your sins may be fun at first; however, they will eventually destroy your life, regardless of what your drug of choice is. It doesn't even have to be a drug. Sin is sin, and the Bible says to be sure your sin will find you out (Numbers 32:23). It doesn't matter what you do or don't do. If you are sinning, you can bet you will have a moment of destruction where you look back and wonder, "How did I get here?" That moment is when you need to have a "come to Jesus" meeting and get right with him. It doesn't matter what you have done or haven't done. God still loves you and cares for you and wants the very best for you.

At some point during my drug years, my mom checked me into a mental health facility here in Tulsa called Laureate. I met a lady there who told me God would never love her again because of the things she had done. Although I didn't know much about God then, I told her it didn't matter what she had done, that he still loved her regardless. She proceeded to tell me that she and a friend had bullied a girl so badly, it made her go legally insane. She was convinced that God could never forgive her.

I am here to tell you: IT DOESN'T MATTER!! You could have killed someone, cheated on someone, stole from someone, etc. And God loves you that much, that He will immediately forgive and forget your sins.

For those of you who have done meth before, you know that it only feels good for a time, and then disaster hits. For those of you who have never done meth, I encourage you to keep reading and see how bad it truly gets. It's not something you want to try. I promise you will be hooked your first time. People use to say stuff like that to me. I never really understood it until I tried it.

By the time I understood, it was too late.

After Oliver moved out of that apartment, he moved back in with his mom for a while, which made things harder on our relationship. Eventually, I got him to get an apartment, but we had to put it in my name because of his failure to pay on the last one. This was a bad decision on my part, but I couldn't see it at the time. I just wanted us to have our own place. For the first few months, I didn't move in with him. I had honestly never really had intentions of moving in with him; I still had a few months left of high school. This caused a lot of fights. He hated staying by himself at night because I would always go home, and he felt like I forced him into this apartment. One day during summer, we were fighting like normal, and I finally gave in and said that I would move in with him. He drove me to my house, we packed up all my stuff while my mom was gone, and I cried the entire time. I knew deep down I was making a mistake. We were so dysfunctional that I knew we wouldn't last, but at least this decision would stop the fight. I was constantly walking on eggshells with him and scared to say anything because I never knew how he was going to react. He was extremely bipolar, manipulative, and controlling.

Again, I just wanted to be loved, and I was willing to do whatever I needed to get it. I just wanted someone to love me the way I deserved to be loved. But what I got was constant ridicule, fights, and controlling behavior. He isolated me from my friends and family to the point where I had no one.

Here's the thing, though: he was broken, I was broken, and when two broken people try to come together as one, you get a big, fat, hot mess. You must become whole by working on yourself before trying to engage in a relationship or marriage. Seek counseling, read Christian self-help books, find out what your problems are, and seek help in those areas, but most importantly, seek out healing from God.

Our fighting continued, which only fueled my need to escape. I started the cycle of going from doctor to doctor trying to get anything I could, from Adderall to Xanax to pain pills. I just needed something to help me get through my days. For the first year or so of my meth use, we only did it on the weekends. I couldn't function correctly after staying up all night, plus we didn't have enough money to keep up the habit throughout the week. So, we would get a sack on Friday night and try to make it last through Saturday. Normally, we wouldn't even make it last through the night. My tolerance kept getting stronger and stronger. When we would start coming down, Oliver would always get so violent. We would start fighting, and of course, everything was my fault. He turned into something I didn't recognize. He was so evil. He would start throwing things, cussing me out, and making me feel like I was worthless. He would constantly threaten me and threaten to take his own life.

It would get so bad.

I can remember one night he got angry at me and took the blow torch and started trying to light the bed that I was laying in on fire. I had been drinking that night, and he was trying to force me to leave, but I knew that I couldn't drive, and a part of me didn't want to leave. Even though I was poorly treated, it was like I was hooked; a better way to say it is that I was addicted to the drugs, to the sex, and to the dysfunction. I was addicted to the drama and addicted to this twisted love. He would flip TVs and punch holes in the walls. He never hit me, but I was always worried that he would. There were times he would speed through neighborhoods and run stop signs, and I would just be holding on begging him to stop. It was violent and traumatic.

Looking back on this behavior and these types of relationships I found myself in, I truly believed it was normal behavior and normal to have relationships like this. Truth is, this behavior is not normal, and relationships like that are not normal. No one deserves to be controlled or manipulated or treated with disrespect. If you find yourself in relationships like what I have been sharing, it's time to re-evaluate things in your life and ask yourself questions like, "Is it worth the turmoil I am experiencing?"

It never mattered how bad it got, though, because, in some twisted way, he ended up feeling bad for what he had done. I would forgive him, and the cycle would just repeat.

We would get another sack on Friday. By Sunday, we were fighting again. He would pack up all his stuff every time and say that he was leaving me, and sometimes he did leave for a little bit but would always return. I would find myself unpacking his things again only for him to repack them up the next weekend and threaten never to come back. It was a constant battle, but my addiction to the drugs and his unhealthy love continued to grow, so it really didn't matter what caused what.

I wanted drugs more than I wanted peace.

He wasn't all to blame in this, either. Yes, he was crazy, but so was I. By this point, my anger from all that I had been through in my past had grown leaps and bounds. I very much had a victim-mentality at the time and thought it was all his fault. However, I can see how I played a huge role too. I would fight back, and I was hateful, hurtful, and rough. I would swing at him and say mean things. I basically fueled the fire.

Our relationship was back and forth. He was bipolar, and my craziness never helped matters any. If he acted crazy, you could bet I was going to act crazier.

He locked himself in the bathroom one night with a bottle of pills and my phone and said that he was going to kill himself. He did things like this often. I believed it the first few times, so much so that I kicked down our bathroom door. When I did, we both just stared at each other in disbelief that I did that, and whatever we were fighting about was over. Our fights never lasted long, but when we fought, it was hard.

We fought hard and loved harder, but it was such toxic love. This was my second relationship full of mental, physical, and emotional abuse. I was beginning to think that this was just normal. I thought all relationships were like this. I grew up seeing my mom yell and throw things, so I honestly thought that this was normal. I had never experienced a good breakup. I thought all breakups consisted of throwing things and yelling at each other, but boy, was I wrong.

God created men and women to love each other, to be there for each other when times are tough, and to hold each other up, not to tear each other down. God did not make us to say hurtful things or even to hurt one another physically. A man is supposed to treat his wife like the princess God has created her to be, to love her as Christ loves the church. On the other side, the woman is supposed to respect and submit to her husband. The man is supposed to be someone that the woman can respect and submit to. You are to both fall in love with Christ and run after Him, and then your relationship will flourish. I heard it put this way. It is as if your love for your husband and God are a triangle. God is at the top of the triangle, and your husband and yourself are on the left and right corners. As you both fall in love with Christ and run after Him, it will bring you two up towards Christ and bonded together the way it was meant to be.

I didn't know any of this. I allowed the cycle to continue, only because I didn't know any better. One night, it got to where I couldn't take it anymore. I went up in our closet and called my mom quietly to tell her I was done. I was scared. I needed her to come to get me and all my stuff. I was terrified of how he would react, so I didn't tell him they were coming. He heard a knock on the door, and when he opened it, my family was standing there. He started yelling, cursing, and throwing things, determined to destroy that apartment since it was in my name. He started smoking cigarettes in the house and putting them out on the carpet. As we packed up all my stuff and put it in the truck, I told my mom to go upstairs and make sure she got all the pills out of the house so that he couldn't do anything stupid. He continued to run his mouth and tell my mom all kinds of stuff I had been doing that she didn't know about. She didn't care at the time, though. We were just concerned with getting all my stuff out of there.

By the time we got home, he was calling and threatening my family and me. My dad got on the phone with him, and Oliver started telling him he was going to come over there and kill him. We had to call the police and have them sent over to the apartment to check on him because he was also threatening to kill himself. This only fueled his anger. He eventually calmed down though and started calling me, apologizing and crying and begging me to come back over. It was like night and day with the flip of a switch.

That relationship lasted for two years. We knew at this point that it was over, but I continued to go over there and hang out with him until he moved out of state. I know you're probably either thinking I am crazy, or you understand the struggle. Like I said before, it didn't matter how bad he hurt me. I kept going back, just like I kept going back to Ryder when he continued to cheat on me.

I was broken and searching for a cure through men.

I didn't know then that man will always fail; God is the only one who can faithfully and fully heal our hearts and put it back together. God is the only man that you can fully trust, never to let you down. God is the only person who can heal your broken heart.

The apartment situation only got worse. It was a disaster. There were about two months left on the lease, which I got stuck paying. He eventually moved to be with family in another state. I was left to pick up the pieces and clean the apartment so I didn't get charged. The maintenance people there were extremely nice and understanding. They knew what I was dealing with, so they tried to help me in any way they could. I was grateful not only for them but also for my friends who came over and helped me clean, paint the walls, and patch up holes in the walls and the carpet.

Even through all of that, I can still see God's hand all over it. It was bad, but it could have been worse in many ways. I ended up getting out of that lease and didn't get charged with anything. Oliver and I continued to talk by phone, but that didn't last long. He was still the same person doing the same things. Once he was out of my life, I swore off meth because I saw what it did to him and me.

Sadly, that didn't last very long.

I want to challenge you. Instead of blaming God for all the things that have gone wrong in your life and asking Him why He wasn't there, I want you to turn it around. I want you to see the good that came out of the bad. I want you to think of how it could have been worse. Just like my last paragraph, I saw how much worse it could have been. I want you to do the same. Make a list if you have to.

It's not that God wasn't there helping you because the opposite is true. God was there. He was helping carry the load of the pain and protect you from it being worse. Even if you were raped, you still have your life. God protected you from dying. There is always a purpose in pain. We go through things, so we can help others come out of the same hurt and pain.

I'm not saying that God causes the hurtful things in life that we go through to happen, but I do believe sometimes He allows it. Like I said before, we live in a fallen world, and people have free will. So sometimes bad things happen to good people, and there is nothing God can do about it. But there is a purpose behind that painful thing. I always say I do not regret anything I have done. I am thankful for every bad thing that happened to me because it has made me the person I am today. Without all that happened to me, I wouldn't be the person I am today.

I hope one day you can turn your pain around for

good. There are plenty of hurting people out there that need to hear your story and need your compassion and empathy to get them through a hard time. People need to hear your story of abuse, neglect, abortion, and addiction. Stop allowing the shame and guilt to hold you back from opening your mouth and telling the world.

There is freedom and healing for others on the other side of your obedience.

Keys to Finding Freedom:

A woman never deserves to be treated this way. I don't care if you hit him first, cussed him out, threw something at him, cheated on him, you name it. A woman never deserves to be beaten or abused in any way. I am not saying that I am condoning a woman behaving that way either. I just want to stress that it is not okay to stay stuck in a relationship where you are being mistreated. You may think he loves you, but if he did, he wouldn't be treating you that way, and that's just the truth. Is it going to be hard to leave him? Yes. But it will be easier in the end if you do it now vs. waiting until it's too late. Trust me when I say, I was in and out of relationships like this for years, and I wish I would have taken them at their words the first time they messed up and hurt me. I was blinded by what I thought was love. I thought they cared for me and loved me and would never hurt me and by the time I saw the real them, it was too late.

Pay attention to the flags! If he starts trying to isolate you from your family or friends, run! Have you heard the saying, "He will treat you how he treats his mama"? That statement could not be more accurate. If your friends and family are coming to you with concerns, listen to them. If you have a gut feeling something isn't right, you are probably right. God made us women to be intuitive; He speaks to us and tells us things. Listen to yourself and those around you who love you. It might just save your life.

My advice for you is if he shows you he can't be trusted, believe that the first time and RUN. It is not worth the pain and heartbreak you will go through in the end if you don't leave now.

> Lord, I pray that You would take the blinders off of these eyes that are reading this right now. That You would show them they are worth more than their circumstances show. They deserve more. God, show them who they are destined to be and help them to see they won't get there if they continue to stay with someone who's unhealthy. Reveal to them the difference between a godly relationship and an unhealthy relationship. Rip the destructive behavior out of them and help them step into what You have called them to be. Give them the strength and courage to walk away when they need to. Help them to stand against abuse and be strong enough to leave the relationship if needed. Father, right now, overwhelm them with Your love and Your desires for them. Show up in their life today and bring a smile to their face.

> In Jesus' name,
> Amen.

CHAPTER 7

Running for My Life

I stayed clean from meth for a little less than a year, opting instead to do just about everything else I could get my hands on. I had found doctors who would prescribe me whatever I wanted. I was labeled with manic depression, ADD, OCD, bipolar, anxiety, and dissociative identity disorder. I took on these labels and lived as if I were these mental health issues. I do believe I had some of the symptoms, mostly due to heavy drug use; however, I fed off these labels. I was disabled in a sense because I had all these mental issues, or so I believed. I am not discounting mental health issues. I do believe these are very real and sometimes require medication. I have had to go through years of anxiety and bouts of depression even after drug use. So, I truly believe there can be chemical imbalances requiring therapy and medication. I am just saying that during those times, I fed into anything anyone would tell me.

They could have told me I was schizophrenic, and I'm sure I would have started hearing voices – you get the picture.

I was vulnerable and willing to take on whatever someone told me. For years, whatever boyfriend I was with, I became like them. I talked like them, I dressed like them, I acted like them. I would even listen and say I loved the same music they listened to. I went through the emo and goth stages; I went through preppy stages and thug stages. I even claimed to be a Juggalo at one point in time. I became whoever I was around. If someone in my group hated someone, I hated them too. If someone loved something, I loved it also. I didn't know who I was, so I masked myself and became whoever I was around.

The addictions continued to escalate. I ended up getting on all kinds of prescription medications and was abusing those as well. I was heavily addicted to pain pills and had a couple of prescriptions to those but still had to buy off the streets. I was sleeping with random guys I had just met and waking up the next morning, not sure who they were. It was a pretty crazy time, and it only got crazier.

I was trying to date a guy who I guess just wasn't that into me. Every time we would start talking, within a week or two, he would stop talking to me. He left me at his apartment one morning when he went to work, and I ended up staying and hung out with some of his friends. There was a guy there who needed a ride home, and we started talking. That same weekend he invited me to go out of town with him to visit a family member of his and to go to some club that was having a rave. I expressed my concerns about meth, and he assured me that it wouldn't be a problem.

However, by the time we got to his family member's house, I found out they were meth dealers. By the end of the night, I was drunk and got offered the pipe and thought, *Why not? It will only be one time.* I couldn't have been more wrong. It was by the grace of God that I was able to walk away from it the first time and stay clean from it for so long. I didn't see it for what it was and was only concerned about having a good time.

After that night, I immediately started craving it every day. It was easy to get because the people I started hanging around with through this guy could always get it. And when they couldn't, they would cook it themselves.

It became an everyday thing.

I couldn't get out of bed without it.

I couldn't go to work without it.

I couldn't function without it.

I had a really good job at the time, but I ruined it with my drug addiction. If I didn't have meth in the morning, I couldn't get up and get ready. I called in a lot. I was also dealing with a lot of health issues, mostly drug-induced, but I felt so bad all the time. If I didn't have the drugs, I couldn't function.

I eventually got fired. I had just bought a brand-new Nissan Altima right off the showroom floor and didn't know how I was going to pay for it. Not long after, I started coming across people who were willing to pay good money for the prescriptions that I had, which turned into yet another addiction – money. I was always on the hunt for something I could flip. I made good money, enough that I was able to keep my car for a while longer. I didn't need a job; selling drugs became my job. I would be in my car from sunup until sundown, and when I wasn't selling drugs, I spent my time at the casino.

The guy that got me back on meth was only around for a few months, but the damage had been done. It's crazy to see how one decision or one person in your circle of influence can completely change the trajectory of your life. Had I never met that guy, would I have gotten strung back out on meth? Maybe so, and maybe not. Up until that point, I was good at telling people no when it came to meth. I had other opportunities to get back into it, but this time everyone was smoking it, so it made it harder to say no. Plus, the lie in my head was so loud that it would only be a one-time thing.

I gave in, and that day, my world began to crash around me. I didn't even see it coming.

Do you see the common thread in my story yet? Relationships. My relationships were terrible, and my life followed that pattern. I was a hurt person attracting hurting people. I was a fixer. I had such a big heart and believed I could fix all these guys without jobs, cars, phones, and houses. I thought I could help them better themselves by getting jobs and money to take care of things. I was wrong. With each relationship, I dug my hole deeper and deeper. I wanted to better them, and instead, they made me worse. Every wrong decision I ever made was because of the influence of someone I was around.

This is why I emphasize that you must guard your heart, your mind, and your life. I've heard people say, "Show me your friends, and I will show you your future." This is so true. Surround yourself with people you want to be like and become.

This whole time, I moved in and out of relationships with all the wrong people, mainly guys who just wanted me to take care of them. I would take care of every need they had, basically becoming their mom. They would just mooch off me and take me for all I had. Looking back on these moments, I think to myself, "How in the world did I allow all of this to happen to me? Why didn't I just say enough and tell them to leave? Why did I continue to allow them to hurt me and use me?"

Because I was lost and broken.

Because I was looking for validation.

I was looking for love to fill a hole in my heart that could only be filled by God.

The addictions only grew worse. I did things I never thought I would do. I ran with people that today I would be afraid of. I was in deep with bad people and every day was a new story of twisted paranoia. I was scared to go outside most days. When I would go outside, I was consumed with paranoia. I swore the police were following me and that there was a group of people following me around just to mess with my head. I got pulled over many times, with all kinds of paraphernalia on me and somehow, they would let me go. I had drug dealers and police officers continually telling me that I didn't belong in the game. When they told me things like that, I would think to myself that they were wrong. I was really good at selling drugs and good at not getting caught. I was able to talk my way out of anything and talk my way into anything. I made really good money. I was able to keep my high every day and those around me high as well. I was able to do all of this and stay out of prison. Everyone around me kept getting popped, but I somehow managed to stay on the streets.

I look back on this now and see God's hand on my life. I look back on moments I walked into houses with straight-up gangster looking dudes. I ran with people in gangs. I was with people making counterfeit money on multiple occasions. I was with people cooking dope.

I should have died.

I should have gotten locked up, but y'all, the grace of God is so thick on my life. I say all the time that there's nothing I could have done to actually kill myself because God stopped the worst from happening every single time.

I continued to follow the path of darkness for seven more years before I decided to get help. For the first three or four years doing dope again, I had no idea I had a problem. I just thought it was a normal life.

I can remember sitting at a close friend's house, and he looked at me and told me straight up, "Rachel, you have a problem. You are addicted."

I was in such disbelief. I have a problem? There's no way!

As I thought about it more, I realized I did have a problem; however, by this point, it was too late. There was nothing I could do to change it. I was accepting the fact that I would probably be an addict for the rest of my life. I can remember sitting in people's houses that were probably in their fifties or later that were shooting up. I remember thinking to myself that this is what my life is going to be like in the future. I am going to be a hoarding IV user for the rest of my life. I had no hope for a better life or a different ending.

Every year brought new situations, new guys, new pain, and new chaos. It was a never-ending spiral that I didn't know how to get out of. I just kept making the same mistakes over and over. I continued to date guys who stole from me, stole from my family, cheated on me, abused me, never really loved me, and only wanted to use me. I would let them live with me. I trusted them, even when they gave me reasons not to. I could never understand how I could love them and do so much for them, and they would just continue to treat me like crap. I still don't understand. When you are addicted to drugs, your morals and values go out the window. The most important thing to you at that moment is finding your next fix, and most will do anything to get it.

I always kept my morals, though. There was a list of things I swore I would never do. I would never prostitute myself for money, I would never shoot up, and I would never steal money from my family. As much as people tried to get me to do those things, I never did. And again, it was all God. When I was with my last boyfriend before going into treatment, he started shooting up at the end of our relationship. I was actually around people who were always shooting up, and it never phased me until one day I wasn't getting high anymore. I was smoking, snorting, and eating meth and nothing was happening. One day, I saw my boyfriend at the time, Logan, shooting up. I was lying on the couch, and he was on the other side of the coffee table. I could see him and his arm through a hole in between the top and the bottom of the table. He had the belt wrapped around his arm and just as he started to put the needle in his arm, I thought to myself, *That needle doesn't look very big, I could probably do that with no problem.* Thankfully, not too long after that day, we split up for good.

CHAPTER 8

In Too Deep

The boyfriend I had before Logan was just as bad, if not worse.

His name was Aiden. He regularly stole drugs and money from me, along with cheating on me and stealing from my family. He took my mom's wedding ring from her jewelry box one day. Boy, that was a hard one to tell her. He pawned it, and we never saw it again. He also stole sentimental rings from me and pawned them too. He would steal my clothes and take them up to the Plato's Closet on the corner. He also put fake scripts in my name, and one time, I had to deal with the police over the whole thing.

I could sit here and tell you stories all day.

I could tell you how bad it was, and how scared for my life I was, but you get it.

Doing drugs seems fun at first, but eventually, it becomes an uncontrollable life. It is not worth it! If you are considering experimenting with drugs, please take my advice. Please learn from my story. It is not worth the pain and trouble it will cause you in the long run. Drugs will take you to places you never imagined.

I am one of the lucky ones. Or I guess I should say, one of the blessed ones. Not all of us make it out. I look up some of my old friends from time to time on Facebook. I have even run into some of them out in public, and most of them are still in it and don't know how to get out.

I have the answer though.

God is the ONLY reason I made it out.

He delivered me and set me free.

Without God, there is no way I would be alive today!

The last couple of years of my addiction were the worst of all ten years combined. They were the scariest and most painful as well. Up to that point, I was just using for fun and didn't realize I had a problem.

At one point, I was running around with a guy who was deeply connected with a gang. He was running drugs for them. Due to the severity of this situation, I am unable to go into a lot of details, and I have changed some of this story and the names to protect the privacy of the people. I was starting to fall for this guy, and yet again, I had fallen for another guy who would want to be with me, but only sometimes. After not hearing from him for a couple of weeks, I found out he was murdered over drugs. This hit home for me. Around this time, my mom had come to me crying because she had found out I was using drugs. I called her that day to tell her what happened, and she said, "Oh my gosh, Rachel, you could've been with him." It was a very chilling moment.

Sadly, it didn't stop me from using. I only spiraled more.

After his death, I continued to go further and further down a deep, dark hole. When I started selling drugs, I was introduced to a man whose street name was something that would have made you cringe. Due to the nature of this person, I can't give you names or details. What I can tell you is, he was a well-known drug dealer who became my supplier. The night I met him was a night I will never forget. This story is one that I don't usually tell and still have a problem with telling to this day. But I am going to say it because you need to know the kind people that are out there and what can happen to you.

We had just gotten home from a long day of pushing his pills. I had helped him sell lots of pills that day, and I was waiting for my cut. He made me wait inside his house for hours while he finished up with his family. When he came inside, he put me in his room while he took a shower. I kept telling him my back hurt. I honestly just wanted some pills. He took it a different way. When he got out of the shower, he came into his room and locked the door. He was a huge guy. Before I knew it, he was on top of me, my dress was off, and his hands were in places they shouldn't have been. I tried to say no, but nothing would come out. I was terrified, and I saw no way out.

My phone started ringing and wouldn't stop, so he threw it to me. I hurriedly said, "We need to hurry and get these pills to this girl before her dad wakes up."

And at that, he got off me, and we went to her house. I still don't understand why he stopped. It's not like this was going to be a big sale. But he did, and I can only thank God for that.

This moment brought so much shame and guilt into my life.

How did I allow myself to get here?

Why was I putting myself in dangerous situations?

Did I need drugs that badly?

I was stunned, in shock, and thoroughly shook up. This just continued the cycle and only made it worse. Life was awful. I was in a severe state of depression, anxiety, and constant paranoia.

While Aiden was living with me, I was seeing another guy on the side, Mason. I wanted to be with Mason, but he was facing prison time. Even after everything that Aiden had done to me, I didn't have the heart to kick him out since he would have been homeless. So, I continued to see Mason and allowed Aiden to continue to live with me. The day Mason got sentenced, I was in the courtroom. He was given ten years. I went home that night and cried and cried and cried until I couldn't cry anymore. That night I took some pills that I thought were Xanax. Come to find out, the Xanax was laced with something. I took two and went to sleep. When I woke up, it was two days later. I woke up to paramedics surrounding my bed and a police officer in the corner with my dope pipe in his hand, asking, "Is this what you are doing?"

I don't remember a lot of what happened next. But my mom told me that I was asleep for two days. She said she came to check on me on the second day and found that my breathing was shallow, and I was pale white. She called a nurse friend of hers to ask her what she should do. Her nurse friend suggested she call 911, so she did. When I woke up, all I remember is my mom trying to get me to go to the hospital to get help. Like I said earlier, I had several health issues we were trying to figure out, and she wanted me to go to the hospital to get tests ran and hopefully find a cure to whatever was making me sick. I honestly believed if they took me to the hospital, they were going to take me to jail. I mean, the police officer already had my dope pipe in his hand. I just knew I was caught and was going to get locked up.

The next few details are hazy for me. My mom helped me fill in the blanks here. My mom had called my dad to come over. I wouldn't listen to my mom, and we kept fighting. My dad asked my mom what she wanted me to do since I wouldn't let the paramedics take me. My mom told my dad that she wanted me to leave. When my dad told me this, I freaked out. I ran out into the living room where my mom was and told her that she didn't know what she was doing. She replied, "I'm not going to let you kill yourself in my house." She proceeded to tell me that she couldn't do it anymore and that I needed to leave. The fighting continued as I frantically tried to pack my things, but apparently, I just threw my belongings all over my room. My mom told me we fought all the way through the house as she was trying to get me to leave. She took my keys to the house and my garage door opener. I left without shoes on, without tampons (I was on my period), without a shower, and without clothes. I had the clothes on my back, my purse, and my phone.

The next two days were a whirlwind of emotions. That night, a friend of Aiden's let us stay at his house. The following day, we went to my house to try to get in so that I could get some of my belongings. All the windows and doors were locked. So, I decided to lay on the front porch until someone came home. I felt so sick that day because I was coming down. I was wrapped up in a blanket lying on the front porch. I can still remember how good the cold concrete felt on my face. At some point, Aiden asked if he could take my car to get us something to eat. I shouldn't have allowed him to, but I did. I had no idea what was to come in the next few hours. As I laid on the porch, I eventually woke up to the sound of the garage door going up. I jumped up and ran around the corner. I slid underneath the garage door as it was going down. I ran into the house, locked myself in the bathroom, and proceeded to take a shower.

When I got out of the shower and walked into my room, I was met with a very distraught Aiden. When I walk into my room, I have a direct shot out the window to the street in front of my house. I saw Aiden sitting in front of my window and just past him, out the window, I could see my car on the street, a total wreck. He had wrecked my car by running into someone. I was livid. I started yelling, cussing, and hitting him. I demanded he get his stuff and leave my house. At this point, my mom had come home. My brother called her to let her know I had made my way into the house. They came back to my room to try and defuse the situation. However, at this point, it was too late.

He grabbed a couple of trash bags full of clothes that he claimed were his and headed out the door. About thirty minutes later, a cop shows up at our house. He proceeds to tell us that Aiden had run into a lady at a stoplight and ran off. The police officer had in his hand a little white case that I kept my pills in. I had just bought twenty pills from someone that I was going to flip and put them in that white case. When the police officer showed me the case, I was nervous. However, when he opened the case to show me what was inside, the only thing left was my ID. Aiden took my car and stole my pills, yet again, to go sell them for his benefit. This only fueled my anger. Aiden had left my ID at the scene with the lady he hit.

The police officer told us a neighbor saw him walking down the street with two trash bags and thought it looked suspicious, so they called the police. He told us that Aiden was currently being detained behind a store around the corner. When we showed up to where Aiden was, he was in handcuffs. He had five warrants out for his arrest in another county, so they were taking him in. The police officers gave us the bags he was carrying. Come to find out, it was filled with my clothes and some he had stolen from others. Remember I told you he had a Plato's Closet hustle? That was precisely his plan with those bags of clothes.

That night, I ended up going out and getting high one more time. My phone was stolen, and the night is a blur. All I know is the next morning, I was dropped off at my mom's house, where I pleaded for her to allow me to move back in. She said she would allow me to move back in, under a couple of conditions, that I stay sober and find a restoration program. So, I came back home and tried my hardest to stay clean. I would love to say it all ended here, but it didn't. In fact, it only got worse before it got better. I stayed sober for twenty-one days. That was the longest I had ever stayed sober. It was awful. I stayed in bed for days. I barely ate. I was sick the whole time.

During the twenty-one days of sobriety, my mom called a married couple who were family friends of ours. This woman is a spirit-filled lady who is on fire for God. She too had a similar past. God delivered her in her jail cell after years of shooting up. My mom thought, if she and her husband would come to pray for me, I would surely be delivered. So, we set up a time for her and her husband to come over. When they arrived, I was nervous. She began to put her hands on my chest and prayed over me. I remember at the time thinking, *This is weird.* She kept saying, "You've got it, there it is." And I kept thinking, *I don't have anything, I have no clue what you are talking about.*

After they were done praying, I didn't feel any different. I still wanted drugs. I still wanted to use. Nothing had changed, and I was disappointed. I remember telling her, "I want God to deliver me as he delivered you in a moment." But he didn't, or at least that's what I thought for the time being. For the next twenty-one days, I tried to stay sober, but it was hard.

You know the saying, "It takes twenty-one days to break a habit"? Well, I was finally starting to feel a little better, enough to where I could get up and get out of the house. I don't know why but, in my head, I thought, *Twenty-one days, huh? I'll show them.* So, on the twenty-first day of my sobriety, I went and got high. This time, it was way worse than before. Everything was heightened. The paranoia was on a new level, the drugs were making me feel crazier than before, and I was quickly spiraling. The reason for this is laid out clearly in scripture. In Matthew 12:43-45, it says, "When an evil spirit leaves a person, it goes into the desert, seeking rest but finding none. Then it says, 'I will return to the person I came from.' So it returns and finds its former home empty, swept, and in order. Then the spirit finds seven other spirits eviler than itself, and they all enter the person and live there. And so that person is worse off than before. That will be the experience of this evil generation."

This is why every time you lay down a vice and pick it back up, it seems like things are worse than they were before. For the next year, I struggled. We started looking for a rehab for me to go to, and I continued to use. I was more scared than before. I was doing things I never thought I would do, even to the point of considering shooting up. I was stealing, lying, cheating, you name it. At this point, all I cared about was getting high. The weird thing was, I wasn't getting high anymore. I was spiraling into a state of sleep deprivation and paranoia, but it wasn't the same anymore. I honestly can't find the words to paint you a picture. Just know that it was terrible. I was hearing things, seeing things, knowing things, and most of the time, I'm not even sure it was real.

My theory on this whole thing was when you fast for God, it opens you up to the spiritual realm. God shows you things and tells you things. When I was using meth, I wouldn't eat for days. In a sense, I was fasting for the enemy. So, of course, I was seeing and hearing things. I also believe that when that lady prayed over me, she imparted the gift of discerning spirits. I had a knowing when things were going to happen, and I could see things in people. If you don't understand this gift and want to know more, I would suggest reading *The Holy Spirit and His Gifts* by Pastor Kenneth Hagin. The gift of discerning spirits allows you to pick up on what kind of spirits are in action in people and certain situations.

During this time, I didn't know that was what was going on, so I was scared out of my mind. This helped fuel my desire to get help. I wanted to hope in the fact that I could live a sober life, but I honestly didn't know if it was going to be possible.

I am so thankful that through Christ, I have been able to find freedom.

CHAPTER 9

Spiraling into the Light

I continued to use for another year.

During that year, we started looking for a place for me to go to get help. My mom told me I had a choice in where I went, and that made all the difference in the world. We went to three different facilities before we found a place that I would call home for the next six months. The place we ended up deciding on is called Mercy Multiplied. We drove to Missouri to tour their home in St. Louis. I remember thinking as we pulled up that the facility was beautiful. We walked in, and I felt such peace. The staff members there were loving and caring. They truly cared about me, and I had only just met them. They walked us around the facility, and inwardly I had a little bit of excitement but also overwhelming fear. When we walked out of Mercy, my mom looked at me and said, "Rach, this is it." I reluctantly agreed with her. All three of us, my mom, my brother, and I had peace about Mercy Multiplied being the facility I should go to. I just wasn't one hundred percent ready mentally to go.

Yes, I wanted to be free.

Yes, I wanted a different life.

But I was scared. This meant leaving the only home I ever knew for six months. This meant finally having to deal with all the pain and suffering I had been through. This meant facing my problems head-on and not hiding behind the drugs. This meant leaving all my friends and completely changing my life.

I was ready, but I was scared. But God helped me.

For the next six months, I dragged my feet. Mercy required me to get all my doctors' records sent to them and to fill out a bunch of paperwork. I also had to do some homework assignments leading up to being admitted into their program. I kept putting stuff off and even told them at one point when they called me with an entry date that I needed to get back on my Xanax and Adderall before I came into their program. This was in October. They told me okay, that was fine, but that they require the girls to be in the house for one month before going home for Christmas break in December. With that rule and me wanting to prolong the inevitable, they told me we would have to wait until the first of the year to bring me in.

By November 1, I was a mess. Nothing I was taking, smoking, snorting, etc. was working anymore. I was in a daze and couldn't function. I knew if I didn't get help soon, I was going to shoot up, and I knew if I shot up, that would be game over. I have always had the mindset that one is good, two is better. My tolerance for medicine has always been high. What worked one day wouldn't work the next day. Knowing this, I knew if I shot up, I would kill myself unintentionally trying to get high. Around this time, God told my mom, too, "If she doesn't get help, she's going to die." My mom has always had the insider info on when people are going to die. She just has a knowing. So, when she came to me and told me this, I was terrified. I didn't want to die.

I ended up emailing my contact person at Mercy and told them I needed to get in and that if I didn't, I knew I was going to die. They called me the next day and told me they would make an exception for me. They told me I had to go to the home in Monroe, LA, and I had to be there next week. I was so torn. I wasn't ready, but I was ready. I knew it was what I needed. I just wasn't sure it was what I wanted. I accepted, and they gave me my date, November 14, 2013. They require that you be sober going into the program. I couldn't stay sober long enough to pass a drug test. Thankfully, I knew someone who worked at a drug testing facility, and she altered my drug test results. She put that I was negative for everything.

The day before I entered Mercy, I did five drugs. The night before, I stayed up all night smoking meth and packing. When the sun started to rise, I began to panic. A friend of mine came over and smoked some weed with me to calm me down. Then I ended up taking a Xanax and went to sleep. The next thing I remember is my mom waking me up and telling me it was time to go. I slept almost the whole way to Louisiana. When I woke up, it was nighttime, and we only had one hour left until we would be at our hotel. That night in the hotel I took a Valium and the next morning I took my last Suboxone. To say I was out of it was an understatement.

I even begged my mom to let me get an alcoholic drink at the restaurant we went to before going to the home, which she did not allow, and I was ticked. I didn't want to face my problems. Nor did I want to stop using, but God helped me submit, buckle down, and stay in the program. When my mom dropped me off at the home, I didn't even cry. I was out of it and was mad at her for leaving me there. I just said goodbye and was fine. It wasn't until hours later, sitting on the floor of the RA's office that I broke down and started crying. The women who staffed this home were like southern mamas to me. The lady helping me check my stuff in will always have my heart. That night, she got on the floor with me and hugged me while I cried. This was just one of many times she intervened as my mama.

That night, they let me go to bed early. The next morning, I woke up and was obviously not feeling good because I was in heavy withdrawal. I asked the staff if I could stay in bed because I didn't feel good. They nicely told me this was a structured program, and if I wanted to stay here, I needed to get up and be a part. I went to the bathroom, and as I was walking out, my counselor met me face-to-face. She proceeded to ask me if I was withdrawing. She already knew what was going on because God had told her. I tried really hard to say no to her, but "yes" came out of my mouth. I just knew I was going to be in trouble. I just knew they were going to kick me out. And I knew my mom was going to be so disappointed in me.

My counselor took me down to the Director's office. When I walked in, I was met with two loving ladies who wanted the very best for me. Instead of being mad at me, they had compassion for me. Instead of telling me to pack my things, they told me to sit on the couch in between them. Instead of asking me questions like, "How could you," they loved on me and prayed for me. They asked if they could put their hands on my back and pray for me. I remember thinking, *Whatever you think will work, go ahead.* At this point, I had tried everything else, and nothing else was working. So, if they thought prayer would work, they could go right ahead. I was skeptical. But what I found was a mighty God who loved me so much that he moved on those ladies' hearts to have compassion for me and pray for me.

As they began to pray over me, they told me to lift my hands in the air. I surrendered to God at that moment. I told God I was tired of doing it my way and that I needed His help. I needed Him to come in and intervene because what I was doing wasn't working. I told Him I was sorry. As I bawled my eyes out, they continued to pray.

This was the moment I recommitted my life to Christ.

When they were done praying over me, I was drenched in sweat. My clothes were literally sopping wet. The director said, "Baby, you need to go change your clothes; you are soaking wet." God detoxed me right there on that couch through those women that day. What would have taken weeks or even months to detox and become normal again, only took one weekend. After they were finished praying over me, they took me to a nearby clinic to have me drug tested. They needed to know what was currently in my system. They honestly had every reason to kick me out, but they decided to let me stay. I'm telling y'all, that was the grace of God. I was so fragile and broken. I was terrified. This was my first time being away from home, and I was states away. God knew I couldn't handle going anywhere else. That day they let me continue to stay in bed and sweat it out. The nurse on staff continued to check on me throughout the day. That night when she came to check on me before she went home, she said my blood pressure was low, and it concerned her, so they took me to the hospital.

I already knew there was nothing a hospital could do for someone withdrawing, but this is where they wanted to take me, so I went. I think they hoped to send me to a treatment facility to allow me to withdraw under the care of people who knew how to deal with people who were detoxing from drugs. However, yet again God intervened. The nurse from Mercy went with me to the hospital. When she asked the nurse at the hospital if I could be sent to a treatment facility, it was the weekend, and they couldn't find me a place to go to. They had no choice but to bring me back to the house and let me detox there. I knew this was God. Going to yet another unfamiliar place with unfamiliar people would have sent me into a massive panic.

The next few days were all God. The day they prayed for me and took me to the hospital was Friday.

Saturday night, I got up and played games with the girls. Sunday, I went to church with them, and Monday, I was up working the program like every other girl. This was God! In the past, I couldn't get out of bed for days, even weeks sometimes. I knew God was working in my life.

Now, I'm not going to say it was easy because it was far from easy. I had to push my way through days of detoxing, sweating, pain, fatigue, sickness, anxiety, fear, and night terrors. I still dealt with all the symptoms and side effects of withdrawing. However, this time was different. This time I had someone by my side, helping me, carrying me, and loving me through it, not just God, but the staff members too.

This started the process of healing. I was in the program for six months, where I received extensive therapy and healing. I had counseling every week, along with reading assignments. Three times a day, we had class, and we were in church twice a week. Altogether, I was engulfed in God. We always jokingly said we were in a "God bubble," but really, we were. I know this may sound extreme to some, but we weren't allowed to watch much TV. We watched Duck Dynasty, football games, and Christian movies. We weren't allowed to listen to any secular music. The meals were strict too. You had to eat a certain amount of food (this was to help those with eating disorders). We could only have sugar once a week. There were many rules that at the time I thought were ridiculous, but looking back on it, I am so thankful for all the rules. I didn't know it then, but I needed structure. I was so used to doing my own thing whenever I wanted. I am so thankful to have been put in a godly bubble because it forced me to spend time with God. It made me read my Bible and forced me to face my problems and work on me with no outside influences.

Through the next six months, I recommitted my life to Christ, I broke soul ties, I received healing from past hurts, I learned how to forgive, I learned how to have a relationship with Christ, and I learned who Christ was and who he created me to be.

I learned relationship and not religion.

God created us for a relationship with Him. As I have spoken about earlier, I thought God was a God of rules and regulations. He just didn't want us to have any fun. That's not what it is about at all. God wants the best for us, and in His best is peace, joy, love, and tranquility. When we step outside of His goodness that He has for us, we experience depression, anxiety, fear, negativity, unworthiness, shame, and guilt. God never intended for us to live a life in fear or insecurity. If we stay connected to God through prayer and His Word, we can find freedom and healing for the pain we have endured throughout our lifetime. God wants to heal you from every hurt. You just have to tell Him you're ready and be truly ready. Don't say you're ready and then take it back, as I did so many times.

Life is truly different now. I am truly different now. My mom tells me all the time how happy of a baby I was. During my drug years, I didn't feel like a happy person. Today, I can now say I have the joy of the Lord. Life is good. God is good. And I will always be thankful for the women at Mercy Multiplied and to God for saving my life.

CHAPTER 10

Freedom Found

Coming home was a whirlwind of emotions. I was excited to be back with my family. But going home meant facing this new life in the same town with the same people. I was scared. The last thing I wanted to do was to run into someone from my past and have to face the dreaded conversation that I was a different person and that I couldn't hang out with them anymore. While I was at Mercy, my family completely redid my room. I gave my mom a list of all the places in my room she needed to check and things she needed to throw away. When I came home, not only did they make sure my room was drug-free, they also took all of my belongings and put it all in the shed. They also repainted, recarpeted, and refurnished my entire room. I was so thankful to come home to what felt like a new beginning.

This is truly where the work started, though. I had

to go through everything that was in the shed. When I opened up the shed, it was like a rush of emotions hit me. I could smell the drugs and the smoke. I could feel the evilness of all my belongings. I know that may sound weird, but I am very much a sensing person, and most of the time, I can feel things before I see them. I was overwhelmed, to say the least. However, I pushed through, and I threw away most of my belongings. I kept only what was necessary and started the process of buying a whole new life.

I had to set many boundaries and put things in place to protect myself. I've seen many women go into rehabilitation programs and come out and run back to the same lifestyle. I believe this is because they have a lack of boundaries in their life, and they don't put the right safeguards in place for their new life. I protected myself every way I knew how, from selling my old phone and getting a new one, deleting my old Facebook and creating a new one, and basically cutting everyone from my past out of my life. This was hard. The friends I was super close with – I had to cut out of my life for good. I told these people I would contact them when I came back, and we'd hang out, and now, this was not something I could do. I didn't know how to handle it, so at first, I didn't. I went to my old Facebook, and before I got on, I went to God. I asked him to shield me and protect me and help me to just immediately deactivate the account without scrolling through the messages and comments. I did just that. I immediately deactivated the account.

When opening up the old Facebook, I was flooded with emotions. I saw my profile picture. I was such a broken little girl. I saw that I had over thirty new messages and too many notifications to count. I had to bypass all that and go directly to my settings and click Deactivate. Once that was completed, I had to make a new Facebook. I prayed and asked God to give me a list of who I needed to block immediately. It doesn't matter how strong you think you are, as soon as homeboy hits you up and you see that message, don't discount how real the enemy is and how real your feelings will be. Because trust me when I say, in my experience, every woman's downfall when it came to not staying sober was because of outside influence. Whether that be a friend or an old boyfriend or even a family member, it doesn't matter. It's essential to make sure when you are trying to better your life that you disconnect and block those that could potentially be stumbling blocks for you in the future – yes, that even includes your family.

Now I know that some of you are reading this are thinking, *Well that's good for you, but my bad influences are my family.* Here's the thing; your freedom is more important than any one person in your life. You are going to have to ask yourself the tough questions. You are going to have to set boundaries. You are going to have to be firm with your loved ones and let them know how you feel. You will have to have that hard talk with them and express your love for them, while also expressing your need for a better life. When you become a different person, most people won't even want to be around you anymore because the Holy Spirit within you is going to be too convicting for them. You may face rejection. Your loved ones may not understand. This is when you have to weigh your options. Is it worth keeping this person in your life and potentially causing you to fall back into the same patterns and routines? Or is it better for you to cut them out in some kind of capacity and keep your freedom?

You don't have to cut them out completely. This is for you to talk to God about and ask him what this looks like for you. Maybe instead of going to their house and spending hours, you just go to dinner for an hour or two. Maybe instead of spending face to face time with them, instead only talk by phone or text. I understand this can be difficult. But again, your freedom is at stake. It's not worth losing the time you have spent bettering yourself. Especially when it comes to old boyfriends. I can't tell you how many times I have seen and heard girls get out of programs and run back to their old boyfriends. Let me save you some time and tell you, IT'S NOT WORTH IT! You will only find yourself back in the same mess you ran to get out of. That is why it is also vital to break soul ties. The reason a lot of women run back to men in the first place is because of a soul tie they have created with them (see resources under Soul Ties for healing at the end of the book).

People are going to show up on your doorstep, they are going to find you on Facebook, you are going to see them out and about if you stay in the same town – that's just part of it. The good news, though, you can be ready. God will help you. Every time you see someone from your past or someone messages you, your immediate response or action should be going to God and asking Him how to handle the situation, as well as asking Him for the strength to handle the situation and the words to say to that person. This is a key component of staying free. Don't just approach the conversation without praying because your emotions and flesh will take over. When you go to God first, He will give you what you need to shut it down.

In November 2019, I celebrated six years of sobriety. Still to this day, I will run into someone, or someone will find me on Facebook from my past. Each time something like that happens, the first thing I do is pray. I ask questions like, Can I respond to them? What do I say? What is my part here? Each time, God has given me the most beautiful responses to people. They are loving, yet firm. I tell people that I love them and always will because I do. I also tell them that I am completely different, and to protect my freedom, I have to keep the past in the past.

Every time I have run into someone in person from my past and talked with them for any given amount of time, all the feelings come rushing back. I end up dealing with all the emotions and memories for days. When I am talking with them, all we can come up with to talk about is the past. This is how I know I can't be friends with people from my past. Again, it's not worth my freedom. Most everyone I have talked with has been understanding. There have been a few that I don't think quite understood. However, not one person has been mean to me about it. For the most part, if people love you like they say they do, they will just be happy you made it out.

While cutting people out of your life from your past should be a top priority, finding a church, small group, and accountability is just as important. When I came home, Mercy required that I have an accountability partner that I met with once a week. I chose to meet with my brother's youth pastor's wife. This sparked a strong friendship between us. Funny story is, before I went to Mercy, both the youth pastor and his wife were the ones who reached out to me most. They chose to pick me as their project if you will. They labored in prayer for me for months and continued to reach out to me by inviting me to events and giving me books and CDs they thought I might like. I make jokes to them because I would come to their youth events in super short shorts. They loved me even with my butt cheeks hanging out.

It's also important that you get plugged into a church. You need good, godly, Christian people surrounding you. You need people that can call you out when they see something isn't right.

This is important!

You may not see it yourself, but those around you will. You have to surround yourself with God because when you come out of that God bubble, it's scary. The world didn't stop while you got free. The world kept evolving and probably got worse. When I got out, I was shocked by the language on TV, the vulgarity of music I used to listen to, and just how people were in general. Although I used to live that life, it felt like I had been this new person for so long it threw me off.

Lastly, reading your Bible every day and spending time with God should be the top priority to you. I tell my ladies I speak to all the time that it doesn't matter if it's only one chapter a day and a quick five-minute prayer, you have to start your day off with God. It sets your whole day up. Reading your Bible is not a thing you have to do to mark off of your to-do list. It's not about seeing how quickly you can read. Reading your Bible is about quality, not quantity. If you can only get through one chapter a day, that's fine. Read it slowly. Ask God questions like, What is this saying? What do these scriptures mean for me? What is my take-away from this chapter? If you don't understand something that you are reading, ask God for clarity. Before you start reading, invite God in. Ask Him to reveal things to you and to help your mind stay focused. When I started doing all of the above, it changed my Bible reading time.

Praying is something you should continually do throughout your day. God created us for a relationship with Him. He wants to hear how your day is going. He wants to hear your thoughts. I fall victim to the thoughts of, *Well, he already saw everything that happened, why do I need to tell him?* Here's why: because a relationship is a two-way street. To hear from God, you have to be talking to Him and have the line of communication open.

God delights in us, and it blesses Him when we take the time to talk with Him, just as you would your best friend. When you call your best friend to tell them what happened to you today like, "GIRLLLL, let me tell you what just happened!!" God wants the same.

So, turn that GIRLLL into GODDDD!

I randomly will ask God for guidance, for help, for comfort, for love, for strength, etc. throughout my day because He is there to help and to listen. If someone hurts your feelings at work, go to the bathroom, tell God about it, and then ask Him to comfort you. Go to Him with everything; that's what he is there for.

These are just a few of the things that I did when I came home from Mercy that made all the difference in the world. I made new friends in new places. The memories from my past were all-consuming at first. I ran drugs all over this town and in surrounding towns. At first, coming home was hard. I couldn't go anywhere without having a bad memory, but it got easier. Eventually, you will have new memories that will overcome the bad.

Here are some things to remember when in the process of getting free.

You are a victor, not a victim.

You are beloved, not unloved.

You are worthy, not unworthy.

You are righteous and redeemed.

You are wanted, cherished, and so ever loved by your Heavenly Father.

God is a restorer of time. It doesn't matter if you're fifty years old and still don't know what you want to do with your life or if you're just now reading this at thirty and realizing you have some healing to go through. I didn't finish my bachelor's degree until I was almost thirty. I didn't figure out what I wanted to do with my life until twenty-six, and I am still figuring it out.

Life is a process.

Healing is a process.

And the process never ends. We will continuously be perfecting ourselves and our lives until the Lord takes us home.

If you ask God what your passions are and what your purpose is, He will reveal it to you.

Is there something that just has your heart?

Something that you get righteously angry about?

Is there something that brings you to tears every time you see it?

Do you see something in your world that could be done better or differently, and you feel like you have the answer? This very well could be your passion and purpose.

Do you have a serving heart and enjoy being there for others?

Are you good at listening?

Do you love kids?

Do you come alive talking to a specific age group or type of person?

Do you have a heart for single moms, widows, orphans, or prisoners?

Ask yourself questions like:

What comes easily to you?

What do you enjoy doing?

What is your heart telling you to do?

What would you do for free?

God has placed a passion and purpose in every person. There is something you are to do to carry out His message and life here on this earth. We are to be an example of Christ's love on this earth. However, when you are born, the enemy wants nothing more than to shut us down and shut us up. The enemy doesn't know exactly what we are going to do in life, but he does see our potential.

I saw a vision one time where God showed me that

those He called had a bright light surrounding them, and this essentially was like a target on their back for the enemy. The enemy wants to shut your mouth and keep you from walking in your purpose. If he can successfully do that, then he has nothing to worry about. However, if His daughters would rise up and step into their God-given purpose and calling, we would be unstoppable. This terrifies the enemy because he knows he will stand no chance.

You should let your past fuel the fire within you to change as many lives with your story as possible. I know it's scary and painful, especially if you are still carrying around shame and guilt, but one in every six women have been sexually abused. There are women out there bound with addictions and issues who don't know how to find freedom. They are holding on to hurt because they don't know how to get free. We have to step up and speak out. We have to tell them how we got free, so they too can receive freedom. I believe that this generation rising up is going to be one of very influential women. We already see it with the multitudes of women preachers on the rise.

The time is here. The time is now.

It is time to receive your healing so that we can bring forth healing to others.

Epilogue

Since graduating from Mercy Multiplied in May of 2014, I have gone on to do great things. I answered the call to go into ministry, started and finished two different schools, and have been actively involved in prison ministry. I went to Victory Bible College in Tulsa, OK, where I studied ministry for two years. I then went on to study counseling at Oral Roberts University for two years, where I graduated with my bachelor's degree. I never thought I was smart enough in high school to even make it to college. I cheated my way through both high school and my associate's degree, so to graduate with my bachelor's was a huge accomplishment. I worked at a restoration program for women here in Tulsa for almost three years called Glory House. This is where my heart truly is, to give back to those as lost in addiction as I was. I am also currently involved in prison ministry, where I get the opportunity to speak, preach the gospel, and minister to those who are lost and hurting.

God is so good. I hope you have found freedom through reading these pages. I truly believe they are God-inspired, just for you. He wants the very best for you, and His very best is for you to be healthy, whole, and healed. I love each and every one of you and will continue to pray over each person who reads this book.

You are in my thoughts, my prayers, and my heart.

Resources

Here is a list of books and teachings I have read throughout the past years that have helped me heal from certain issues. I have labeled each resource, so you can easily find what you are struggling with and read or listen to the corresponding book or teaching.

Insecurity
Captivating by Stasi Eldridge & John Eldridge

Rejection
Uninvited by Lysa TerKeurst

The Root of Rejection by Joyce Meyer

Childhood Wounds
Father Wounds: Reclaiming Your Childhood by Francis Anfuso

Comparison
The Comparison Trap by Andy & Sandra Stanley

Soul Ties/Toxic Relationships
Soul Ties by Frank Hammond

No More Sheets by Juanita Bynum

Relationship Goals by Mike Todd

Keep Your Love On by Danny Silk

Thoughts/Mind Wars
Battlefield of the Mind by Joyce Meyer

Winning the Mind Wars by Steve Berger

Addiction/Cutting/Inner Healing
Trapped by Nancy Alcorn
(Drug Addiction)

Mercy Moves Mountains by Nancy Alcorn
(Stories of overcoming life-controlling issues)

Echoes of Mercy by Nancy Alcorn
(Stories of overcoming life-controlling issues)

Ditch the Baggage by Nancy Alcorn
(Inner Healing)

Cut by Nancy Alcorn
(Self-Mutilation)

Starved by Nancy Alcorn
(Eating Disorders)

Approval Addiction by Joyce Meyer
(People pleasing)

Physical and Sexual Abuse
"One Life" by Joyce Meyer

Violated by Nancy Alcorn

Beauty for Ashes by Joyce Meyer

Anger
Managing Your Emotions by Joyce Meyer

Being Filled with the Spirit/Closer Relationship with God
The Spirit Within and the Spirit Upon by Kenneth Hagin

Practicing His Presence by Frank Laubach
Filled with the Holy Spirit by Joyce Meyer

Heaven is for Real by Todd Burpo

The Purpose Driven Life: What on Earth Am I Here For by Rick Warren

Authority/Speaking Over Yourself
The Secret Power of Speaking God's Word by Joyce Meyer

God's Creative Power by Charles Capps

God's Creative Power for Healing by Charles Capps

The Believer's Authority by Kenneth Hagin

The Power of the Blood by H. A. Maxwell Whyte

Setting Boundaries
Safe People: How to Find Relationships That Are Good for You and Avoid Those That Aren't by Henry Cloud & John Townsend

Boundaries: When to Say Yes, How to Say No To Take Control of Your Life by Henry Cloud & John Townsend

Unforgiveness
Dealing with Offense by Joyce Meyer

Total Transformation by Joyce Meyer

Your Past, Your Future, Your Choice by Nancy Alcorn

"The Poison of Unforgiveness" by Joyce Meyer
    https://joycemeyer.org/everydayanswers/ea-teach-ings/the-poison-of-unforgiveness

Acknowledgments

It took me almost seven years to finally get this story on paper and in book form. I had many people telling me for years that I needed to write my story out into a book. I started it when I came home from treatment. I wrote five chapters over two years. I thought I had lost the book when my flash drive was stolen, but it popped up a couple years later on a computer I must have saved it on. That's when I knew I was supposed to write this book.

First, I want to thank my family, especially my mom and grandma, for never giving up on me. They relentlessly pursued me to no avail. On multiple occasions, they bailed me out of bad places and prayed tirelessly. They never turned their backs on me, and they loved me regardless of my actions.

I want to thank my brother, who had open arms for me when I came home like nothing ever happened.

Thank you for always pushing me to be better, being patient with me, and caring for me like you do.

Lastly, I want to thank all of those who helped shape and shift me into the woman that God has called me to be – the staff members at Mercy Multiplied, the teachers and friends at Victory College, staff members at Glory House, and friends and professors at Oral Roberts University.

This has been a long process, but I am thankful for each of you who have helped this book become a reality.

Invite Rachel to Speak

When you invite Rachel to speak to your church or event, be prepared to laugh, cry, and hear spiritual truths from the Lord. Rachel is committed to hearing the voice of the Lord for her audience and being obedient to what he puts on her heart to share. She can break things down practically for application and has the ability to allow her audience to see spiritual truths in a different light.

To book her to come speak for your church service or event, you can contact her by email at daringtolivefree@gmail.com.

To keep up to date with what Rachel is doing, follow her on Facebook by searching "Dare to Live Free."

Made in the USA
Las Vegas, NV
29 September 2021

31344558R00069